Elisa Alberto   Christine Wawra

MAKING VIRTUAL REAL

HOW TO LEAD GLOBAL TEAMS ACROSS DISTANCE

Copyright Statement

All of the information and material inclusive of text, images, logos, product names is either the property of, or used with permission by the authors Christine Wawra and Elisa Alberto. The information may not be distributed, modified, displayed, reproduced – in whole or in part – without the prior written permission of Christine Wawra and Elisa Alberto.

Disclaimer

The information contained in this book is compiled from various sources and provided on an "AS IS" basis for general information purposes only without any representations, conditions or warranties whether express or implied, including any implied warranties of satisfactory quality, completeness, accuracy or fitness for a particular purpose.

Christine Wawra and Elisa Alberto and related corporations ("Doujak Corporate Development") disclaim any and all liability for all use of this information, including losses, damages, claims or expenses any person may incur as a result of the use of this information, even if advised of the possibility of such loss or damage.

© Christine Wawra & Elisa Alberto 2016

Cover illustration Copyright © 2010 by Susanne Hun

Cover design by Susanne Hun

Book design by Susanne Hun

Published by Amazon

Editing by Judith Tavanyar

Chapter illustrations © see references

"Global leaders have to deal with a new complexity coming from working virtually and leading virtual teams. Making Virtual Real is a great guide that will help you to reflect on the leadership skills needed in this new virtual world!"

Stanislaus Turnauer, Owner and CEO Constantia Industries AG

"Whether you are part of a geographically dispersed team or leading a global team, Making Virtual Real provides you with easy-to-read information, tools, and techniques for successfully navigating across cultures and distance. Having the right technology in place will not make you an effective virtual team: you have to know how to use it and how to foster social interactions in the virtual space".

Eva Maria Bieda, Director Global Business Communication, Dow Chemical Company

"How to be able to constantly maintain trust and motivation when dealing with a virtual team made of 20 nationalities spread across 15 European countries? This has been my challenge for many years. 'Making Virtual Real fosters understanding how to lead this kind of team and it's a helpful tool to better manage international talents in any company".

Matteo Ferrazzi, Head of Strategy and Business Communication, Unicredit Group

"Making Virtual Real is a great source for any leader managing global virtual teams. It provides concrete tips for building trust and enabling collaboration in virtual teams, and covers the topic of culture and the intercultural challenges arising when working virtually".

Martina Ernst, Head of HR, Erste Bank der österreichischen Sparkassen

"For anyone leading teams across geographies Making Virtual Real is a must. This book provides anyone dealing with the complexity of virtual teams with indispensable insights on virtual team dynamics and virtual leadership. It is full of practical tips for enabling and supporting your people to work together effectively in today's global workplace".

    Martin Kussner, Strategic Planning Europe, Middle East & Africa, DuPont de Nemours

"Virtual collaboration is one of the most underestimated barrier in increasingly global and complex organisations and value chains. Elisa Alberto and Christine Wawra treat all dimensions of virtual collaboration in a very viable way."

    Alexander Gisdakis, Consultant, Strategytopeople

"Making Virtual Real provides many specific examples on common pitfalls, how to avoid them as well as how to enhance virtual collaboration overall. There is something in it for everybody, from the experienced virtual global leader to the rookie. For somebody constantly working in multicultural and virtual settings like me, definitely a worthy read!"

    Stefan Ulrich, Consultant at The Boston Consulting Group

"Working in virtual teams is the key to navigate through the challenges of the new economic speed, made of spaces and times that are constantly changing. Companies started to be aware of that. Virtual working itself is a challenge, requiring people to develop new competences through appropriate training"

    Daniele Mazzi, Country Controller ABB Italy

ACKNOWLEDGEMENTS

This book has been a major work that has been possible only thanks to the people who have supported us and believed in it.

First of all, thank you to Alexander Doujak for having supported us throughout the compilation of the book and for the opportunities for us to 'learn by doing' in the projects in which we are involved at Doujak Corporate Development.

To Susanne Hun, our amazing graphic designer, who has patiently supported us in turning words into a story. Her creativity and professionality brought this book to a next level.

To Judith Tavanyar, our fabulous editor, who has done terrific job in not just editing this book with preciseness, creativity and professionality but in giving us also content advice, being herself an expert on the topic of virtual leadership and virtual collaboration.

To Elisabeth Babnik, who has been a major support in getting this project done and has motivated us right up to the last mile to accomplish this small dream.

To Marc Sniukas, who started the whole virtual collaboration topic at Doujak internally (together with Christine Wawra), and who constantly supported us with his advice and with the development of the virtual team assessment tool we discuss in this book.

To Aidan Bruynseels and Viviana Rojas de Amon, who played a major role early on in conducting the survey and interviews with virtual teams that brought this book to life.

TABLE OF CONTENTS

ACKNOWLEDGEMENTS   5

FOREWORD   8
- **ABOUT THIS BOOK**   8
- **SO WHAT ARE YOU INTERESTED IN?**   10
- **ABOUT THE AUTHORS**   14
- **ABOUT DOUJAK CORPORATE DEVELOPMENT**   15

CHAPTER 1 INTRODUCTION   16
- 1.1. AN INTRODUCTION TO VIRTUAL TEAMS   16
- 1.2. ADVANTAGES OF VIRTUAL TEAMS   18
- 1.3. CHALLENGES FOR VIRTUAL TEAMS AND HOW TO TAKE ADVANTAGE OF THEM   22
- 1.4 MANAGING RELATIONSHIPS AND TASKS – WHAT VIRTUAL TEAM LEADERS NEED TO KNOW   30

CHAPTER 2 THE IMPLICATIONS OF CULTURE IN CROSS-CULTURAL VIRTUAL TEAMS   36
- 2.1. WHY IS CULTURE IMPORTANT?   37
- 2.2. INTERCULTURAL DIFFERENCES THAT HAVE AN IMPACT IN VIRTUAL TEAMS   45
  - COMMUNICATION: WHEN IS IT TIME TO TALK AND TIME TO BE SILENT?   47
  - FEEDBACK: TO WHAT EXTENT IS COMMUNICATING DIRECTLY 'CRITICAL FEEDBACK' ACCEPTABLE?   54
  - TIME: HOW DO DIFFERENT PERCEPTIONS OF TIME AFFECT TEAM COLLABORATION WHEN WORKING VIRTUALLY?   61
  - RELATIONSHIPS: WHAT IS NEEDED TO BUILD AND MAINTAIN TRUST?   66

CHAPTER 3 LEADING HIGH-PERFORMING VIRTUAL TEAMS.   72
- 3.1. THE ROLE OF THE LEADER   72

	3.2.	BUILDING THE VIRTUAL TEAM	78
		TOOL: SAMPLE PROCESS FOR BUILDING A TEAM	80
		CASE STUDY: "BUILDING UP A GLOBAL VIRTUAL TEAM"	100
	3.3.	GUIDELINES FOR LEADING VIRTUAL TEAMS	102
	3.4.	ASSESSING YOUR VIRTUAL TEAM PERFORMANCE	114
		VIRTUAL TEAM PERFORMANCE SELF-ASSESSMENT	116
		VIRTUAL TEAM PERFORMANCE ONLINE-ASSESSMENT	132
CHAPTER 4 VIRTUAL MEETING FACILITATION			**134**
	4.1.	MASTERING THE TECHNOLOGY	134
		CHOOSING THE RIGHT VIRTUAL MEETING TOOL	136
		USEFUL TIPS BEFORE THE SESSION	140
		PREVENTING AND DEALING WITH PROBLEMS	142
	4.2.	ROLES AND FEATURES IN VIRTUAL MEETINGS ROLES IN A VIRTUAL MEETING	144
		VIRTUAL FEATURES	146
	4.3.	VIRTUAL MEETINGS IN PRACTICE	148
		PREPARATION – DESIGNING THE VIRTUAL MEETING	152
		WARM UP	158
		THE CONTENT, TIME, SPACE AND SOCIAL DIMENSION	174
		WRAP UP	183
		FOLLOW UP	187
CONCLUSION			**190**
REFERENCES			**192**

FOREWORD

ABOUT THIS BOOK

A quick word about why we decided to write this book for anyone working in or leading a remote team, or who may be interested in doing so. So firstly, a bit about us. Our own team at Doujak Corporate Development is spread all over the world, and we take advantage of this! Not having to sit in an office, but rather use the talents (wherever in the world we may find them) that fit our company and projects the best is a huge advantage to our business. We only meet twice a year for our summer and Christmas workshops; time that we use for working on our strategy, reviewing projects in the pipeline but also for further personal development and teambuilding. As for everything else - the rest of our collaboration happens mostly online and occasionally jointly, on site with the client. Indeed, virtual collaboration in general is now a key part of our work with clients and increasingly a vital element of international change projects.

We have learned over the years that performing well as an international team is not only about having the right technology in place, but also understanding the 'interpersonal dynamics' of working virtually, and what makes that a special and different experience from working face to face. This book is a compilation of 7 years of practice and research in the field of leading virtual teams and virtual collaboration, and in it we share practical tips, ideas and research findings to help you understand these key elements of the virtual approach, and adjust them to your own needs as a remote team leader, consultant or trainer.

In many ways virtual leadership has become not just a cornerstone of our business but also a professional passion for both authors. Nevertheless, the impetus to write this book began right back in 2009, when we — Elisa Alberto and Christine Wawra — started a research project at our company, Doujak Corporate Development, focusing on what it means to work internationally. The aim was to identify the top challenges and best practices managers and consultants working internationally were facing in their daily lives, and to think about solutions on how to address them.

We started with a qualitative survey consisting of face-to-face and telephone interviews, later backed in 2010 by an online questionnaire to deepen our results. What did the survey tell us? The results showed that building trust in international/dispersed teams and leading virtually were some of the biggest challenges to corporate leaders, which reaffirmed our own experience when working with numerous change management and team development projects over the years. Further challenges which the survey highlighted as common experiences in working internationally were:

- time differences
- linguistic difficulties
- the 'unevenness' of skills across borders
- finding ways to synergize national, professional and local cultural differences among members into a single, coherent and high-functioning team.

As a further step, we decided to do a deep dive into why these challenges exist, and what possible solutions may be found. In 2011, we ran a second survey, this time focusing on the experiences, tendencies and constraints that might emerge when working as a member or leader in virtual teams, and a key finding highlighted by this study was the importance of working collaboratively in virtual teamwork. Over time, we found ourselves using more and more virtual tools for facilitating the change processes and assignments we were working on as consultants, and at the same time, continued to develop new concepts and best practices in leading global virtual teams.

Finally, our Doujak Global Survey in 2014 showed that for many businesses, the topic of virtual collaboration is still a significant challenge, and getting it right is a powerful success factor for leaders running international projects. The recently published results of the Doujak Global Survey 2016[1], conducted with more than 400 managers of leading international companies, has shown that digital transformation is perceived as one of the top 5 challenges in 2016 and now therefore plays an important role on the leadership agenda.

These conclusive findings made us realise that it was finally time to publish the knowledge we had gained from our research and experience. The result is this book.

1 Doujak Global Survey 2016: http://www.doujak.eu/insights-publications/the-doujak-global-survey-2016/ (seen January 2016)

FOREWORD

SO WHAT ARE YOU INTERESTED IN?

- Do you ever ask yourself what a virtual team really is and what it is useful for? If you are interested in this, and why on earth it is so challenging to work in a virtual team, then **CHAPTER 1** is a good starting point for you.

- Are you interested in finding out more about the implications of 'culture' in cross-cultural virtual teamwork, perhaps so that you can better understand your colleagues and team dynamics in general? Then you should find some great tips in **CHAPTER 2**.

- As a leader of a virtual team yourself, you may be wondering what will be expected of you and what you can do to build trust and keep motivation high in your team? Then you might want to browse **CHAPTER 3**, which includes a sample process on how to build a virtual team, as well as a case study to consider.

- Perhaps you already have some experience in leading virtually, but are concerned that your meetings are often boring or inefficient, or even ruined by technical setbacks? Virtual meetings of course play an invaluable role in leading across distance.
CHAPTER 4 addresses this key issue by providing general information on choosing the right tools for your meetings. It also gives 'hands on' tips on how to facilitate virtual meetings, supported by anecdotes and insights from our experience of running virtual change management projects.

CHAPTER 1: INTRODUCTION

The first Chapter aims to give you an insight into virtual working and what makes it unique and different from teamwork that takes place in the co-located environment.

- We consider here what makes virtual teams special, highlight their benefits and challenges, and discuss how to best use the potential they offer.
- We look at the four types of distance that arise in virtual teamwork (physical, social, cultural, technological) and discuss what a leader or team member could do to overcome them.
- As a virtual team leader or team member, you become more aware of the importance of considering both task and relationship issues that have an impact on individuals, teams and entire organisations when people work together across distance.

CHAPTER 2: THE IMPLICATIONS OF CULTURE IN CROSS-CULTURAL VIRTUAL TEAMS

Culture plays an important role in the virtual context as much as when working face to face and clearly influences communication and interactions within a virtual team. In this Chapter we look at the theme of culture, and provide you with a practical tool (our culture model) to analyse it. In doing so, we explore in more depth some specific topics that have an impact in cross-cultural virtual teams.

- We highlight the different communication styles that can develop and make an impact in cross-cultural work, and look into appropriate ways of managing different preferences regarding aspects such as 'small talk' and 'conversational turn-taking' among your own team members from different cultural backgrounds.
- We discuss how to give (critical) feedback in an intercultural virtual environment and work with varying individual expectations and preferences when giving and receiving feedback.

FOREWORD

CHAPTER 3: LEADING HIGH-PERFORMING VIRTUAL TEAMS

As Caulat points out: "the crucial differentiator between mediocre and high-performing virtual teams is the development of virtual leaders who are able to develop and lead virtual teams. Effective management of virtual teams is necessary but not sufficient: there is a real need for virtual leadership"[2].

- In this Chapter we explore in more depth the role of a virtual leader and share some insights on the multiple aspects of that role. After reading this, you gain awareness of the broad-ranging competences that are required to lead well when you are not sitting in the same office as your team members. These include, but are not limited to, skills in managing technology, interpersonal and intercultural effectiveness, communication and management. In addition, we highlight the clear need to build trust and collaboration in a virtual team by encouraging you to share information, learn from each other, motivate team members and generally enhance relationships within the team.

- A sample 'process' for team leadership is offered here, and from this and the Case Study we also provide, you get some ideas on what it takes to build a strong virtual team.

- The nine guidelines for leading virtual teams offer you clear practical tips to apply straightaway.

- Finally, assessing your team performance – this Chapter helps you to do so effectively.

---

[2] G. Caulat, "Virtual Leadership", The Ashridge Journal, Autumn 2006.

CHAPTER 4: VIRTUAL MEETING FACILITATION

In any discussion about virtual collaboration, it is essential to mention virtual meeting facilitation. One of the key elements of virtual facilitation is, of course, the technology which makes it possible to communicate with colleagues across distance. After reading our final Chapter, we aim to make you feel well-informed and more confident, so that you:

- Know how to master the technology by choosing the right virtual meeting tool for the desired outcome of the meeting (meeting purpose) and according to the specific needs of your audience (including number of participants)
- Know how to prepare the appropriate technical set up for your virtual meetings and training events
- Know useful 'back up' strategies to keep on hand when faced with technical problems during your session – and also how to prevent them in the first place
- Know the varying 'roles' and responsibilities that virtual meetings demand of us, and how to make use of the different features of virtual platforms to help us best fulfill those roles
- Learn about the practical checklists that are helpful to get you set up and be confident in running powerful and effective virtual meetings and events in general.

After reading this book, we hope that you will feel inspired to take ahead some ideas and practices from it into your daily work as you explore further this question of **"how to make virtual real"**.

FOREWORD

ABOUT THE AUTHORS

ELISA ALBERTO is partner at Doujak Corporate Development. Elisa's work focuses on global change management projects; organisational transformation and culture change; development and implementation of change communication strategies; international collaboration and team development; in virtual as well as face to face settings. She also coaches managers and executives on intercultural challenges, from one-to-one coaching to designing and delivering multinational and virtual team building programs, as well as global leadership and intercultural trainings. She has extensive experience in the field of virtual teams and virtual collaboration and is also a certified virtual trainer. Originally from Italy, Elisa has lived in several countries: USA, France, Spain, the Netherlands, Denmark, Austria and currently lives in Munich, Germany.

CHRISTINE WAWRA is partner at Doujak Corporate Development. Her main areas of expertise are international change management and transformation projects as well as strategy development and implementation projects with a focus on leadership, involvement and communication. Christine is an expert in executive team development and coaching and the design and delivery or large group events. She has extensive experience in the field of virtual teams and virtual collaboration in terms of consulting and training. Born and raised in Austria, Christine has travelled around the globe for work assignments, as well as for pleasure: at the time of publishing this book, she has been to 44 countries on four continents, inspiring her work and her thinking for this book to a considerable degree.

ABOUT DOUJAK CORPORATE DEVELOPMENT

DOUJAK CORPORATE DEVELOPMENT is a boutique consulting company partnering with CEOs, executive teams and owners of Fortune 500s and Hidden Champions to resolve the global strategic and organisational challenges they face. We use strategic problem-solving, innovative thinking on management and leadership, and pragmatic insights about people and organisations to help our clients shape strategy and develop the capabilities and organisational culture, structure, processes, systems and leadership needed for global execution and business transformation.

The consulting services range from individual 1-on-1 coaching session, and working with management teams, right through to steering global initiatives and establishing long term corporate development functions. In any scale of project, we keep a focus and channel our deep expertise on strategy, change management, communication, professional development, leadership and facilitation.

Besides the main office in Vienna, the Doujak team is spread all over Europe and US (Munich, Frankfurt, Zurich, Luxembourg, Berlin, New York).
For further information, visit: www.doujak.eu

CHAPTER 1 INTRODUCTION

1.1. AN INTRODUCTION TO VIRTUAL TEAMS

What is the first thing you do when you start your working day? Most likely it is turning on your computer, logging in into your company's virtual platform or checking your e-mails on your smartphone. Probably while reading this book you may be also receiving e-mails from your colleagues in China or perhaps waiting to join a web-meeting with your US partners. This new "working approach" of being constantly and easily reachable through different media not only has become a requirement for executives right across the world, but it is also now a key priority for businesses of all shapes and sizes to be able to minimize cost structures in order to maximize return on capital. Virtual teams are one way of reducing travelling costs, while hiring top talent, irrespective of location in the world.

The "traditional" way of working – going to the office and seeing your colleagues face to face – is, increasingly, in decline. In its place, we see a new way of working, which not only opens up numerous opportunities but also takes full advantage of recent technological developments. People working in virtual teams are usually highly reliant on electronic communication; some team members may even be entirely dependent on IT, never communicating with their colleagues outside the Internet meeting or phone conference. And even those employees who still have a job where they go to the office every day and meet colleagues face to face, will almost undoubtedly also have some regular 'virtual' conversations in order to get their daily jobs done. When you think about what the word 'team' means to you, you might find yourself agreeing with the following statements made by Mabey and Caird[3] enriched with our own experience:

- A team consists of at least two team members
- A team is a group of people who share a common purpose
- The team members contribute to achieving a joint goal, bringing in their skills and capabilities
- The team has its own 'team identity'
- The team develops communication patterns internally and with the external world
- The structure of the team is based on goals and tasks
- The team continuously works on its own efficiency and performance

A virtual team is no different. It just works via a different channel of communication to achieve its purpose.

---

[3] Christopher Mabey and Sally Caird 1999 Building Team Effectiveness Open University, Milton Keynes, ISBN 0-7492-9553-8, Page 7 ff.

As we've suggested, using 'virtual tools' such as e-mail, online-platforms or webinars, holds many advantages and opens up a whole lot of new opportunities, not only in terms of saving cost for your business. Accessing talent by becoming independent from the constraints of geographical location and thus being able to work with whoever suits the position best, is, of course another benefit. Wikipedia[4] gives a definition of virtual teams which summarises our view perfectly:

> *A virtual team (...) is defined as a group of individuals who work across time, space and organisational boundaries with links strengthened by webs of communication technology.*

Perhaps at this point it's important to be clear about our definitions. Virtual teams are, of course, commonly also global teams – ie teams working right across the world - but they don't have to be. The key point here is: virtual teams are formed whenever working from different locations is necessary, regardless of how far those locations actually are from each other, and as long as the main communication channel is virtual. In contrary to the virtual team, a global team by definition has to be international – meaning you and your two colleagues in London working via GoToMeeting makes you properly virtual, but not quite global yet.

[4] https://en.wikipedia.org/wiki/Virtual_team (14.7.2015)

CHAPTER 1 INTRODUCTION

1.2. ADVANTAGES OF VIRTUAL TEAMS

As we've suggested, the advantages of virtual teamwork are considerable, often entirely offsetting the set up costs – such as IT software installation and licensing, training and so forth. However, a couple of provisos should be highlighted here. Firstly, for virtual teamwork to be successful, organisations need to be aware of best practices for the use of virtual technology. Secondly, virtual teams need to exist in an organisational culture that fully supports this way of working. If these two provisos are not fulfilled by the organisation, this might require more co-ordination and work from the team leader and the team members - particularly in the 'team set up' phase, which should involve choosing the virtual technology and getting going with it, as well as defining virtual team culture and how it will be linked to the rest of the organisation.

One of the key advantages of virtual working is that managers can build teams with personnel from all over the world and source expertise from wherever they are located to troubleshoot global or local problems. This helps to break down organisational barriers and lowers operating costs whilst increasing collaboration. The heterogeneous mix of the teams in terms of cultural background, expert knowledge, regional know-how and local working practices is especially diverse in most virtual teams and therefore can be very advantageous.

SO WHAT ARE THE OVERALL ADVANTAGES OF VIRTUAL TEAMWORK?

In the table on the right we have clustered some of the benefits into three sections: organisational, team and individual advantages. Bear in mind when reading this that these advantages are not necessarily immediately noticeable, and are not automatically guaranteed unless they are supported by effective choice and use of technological tools, and a supportive culture which enables people to implement virtual working smoothly and confidently.

ORGANISATIONAL ADVANTAGES	TEAM ADVANTAGES	INDIVIDUAL ADVANTAGES
• Breakdown of organisational barriers
• Lower operating costs
• Increased collaboration
• Increased international alignment
• Responding faster to market changes
• Benefitting from time shifts 24/7	• Members can focus on their job and are less disturbed
• Working times are more flexible
• Less travelling /save on travelling costs
• Shorter meetings, higher efficiency	• Team variety: source expertise from anywhere in the world
• International and intercultural exchange that foster creativity and innovation
• Use of individual strengths and talents at their best
• No need for all team members to be present together
• Better work-life balance, reducing travelling & commuting times
• More flexibility in work and private life

Fig. 1: Advantages of Virtual Teams. © Doujak Corporate Development

CHAPTER 1 INTRODUCTION

ORGANISATIONAL ADVANTAGES

In many multinational organisations with different departmental functions spanning continents, the need for collaboration can be costly and time-consuming. It can also make a large corporation significantly less mobile and agile than its smaller competitors as it may take far more time to review existing products and services and, generally, to innovate.

Here are some of the advantages at organisational level of using virtual teams within the corporate structure:

- Reduction of organisational barriers and thus increased accessibility to personnel on all levels.
- Increased cross-functional collaboration between different members of the same organisation, no matter the geographical distance between them, and at a low cost – research and development executives can now work more smoothly and cost-effectively with, say, sales teams, and so forth.
- Increased accessibility/availability of management support, leading to increased trust and cooperation in general between team members and their leaders.
- Travelling time and cost is reduced significantly, saving vast amounts of capital, and lowering operating costs also, as far less employee time is spent away from base.
- Differences of time zone become less significant when effective communication via online media means that personnel spread over distance can work within their own time zones, without having to travel to collaborate. This not only reduces travel time but also jet lag and related stress and fatigue, and maximises individual effectiveness.

TEAM ADVANTAGES

One of the key advantages which global virtual teams bring to an organisation is that of diversity. In other words, due to the cross-functional and cross-cultural nature of the geographically-spread team, a very real benefit emerges - the decisions made by that team are more likely to have global 'reach' and relevance than in a co-located, geographically intact team. Here are some further advantages:

- Expertise can be gleaned from all over the world at any one time, whether it is technological innovation in one country or management in another.
- Virtual teams can stimulate international and intercultural exchange of contacts as well as ideas, resulting in increased development of external networks for customer-focused companies.

- There is no requirement for everyone to be present in the same time zone at the same time, thereby removing the need to complete the logistical nightmare of a global meeting with its time and cost implications.
- In project teams located across the globe, virtual working enables 24/7 continuation of effort. While one team member might have just finished her working day, another one is just starting hers, and can 'pick up' and continue the work where her team member left off. If well-coordinated, this round-the-clock team input can be a truly huge advantage.

INDIVIDUAL ADVANTAGES

For individual team members, there is a similarly impressive list of advantages in virtual teamwork. They include:

- A massive reduction in 'down time' or travel hours previously wasted sitting in the plane or in the car on the way to the next meeting.
- Very often, web meetings are shorter than face to face ones and also sometimes more effective in achieving their purpose. Web-meetings in general should not last longer than 90 minutes because they require a higher level of attention and therefore are often also perceived as more tiring. Keeping the focus on – say - 60 minutes of virtual working at full speed, with everyone focusing on the task in hand can sometimes therefore bring better results than the face to face meeting which lacks that focus.
- Increased effectiveness of team collaboration gives individual team members more time to focus on their work without being disturbed, in turn enabling a higher level of self-organisation, autonomy and flexibility.
- Virtual team work in general can also offer a better work-life balance for those concerned, offering the possibility of working flexibly from home, and/or in part-time hours more easily. This can be a strong motivator (and performance enhancer) for team members who have family commitments, for example, and who can work more consistently and productively without needing to travel to an office base or do a full week's work within proscribed office hours. Virtual working generally provides better work opportunities, as personnel working across distance are no longer confined to looking locally for a role, but can consider a whole range of possible posts with job specifications that suit their interests and skills.

CHAPTER 1 INTRODUCTION

1.3. CHALLENGES FOR VIRTUAL TEAMS AND HOW TO TAKE ADVANTAGE OF THEM

It's interesting that many managers perceive a big difference in the leadership skills that are required when managing virtual teams, because when we look at the main success factors for any team –such as achieving tasks to deadline and on budget, enabling communication or dealing with conflicts, there are some basic elements which are clearly of equal importance for both local/face to face and geographically dispersed/virtual teams. At the same time, aspects of teamwork such as team size, skills and competencies of team members, social dynamics between team members – all these will affect the performance of any team, no matter whether it operates virtually or through face to face presence.

SO WHAT ARE THE CHALLENGES SPECIFIC TO VIRTUAL TEAMWORK OF WHICH TEAM LEADERS AND MEMBERS NEED TO BE AWARE WHEN WORKING ACROSS DISTANCE?
To a large extent, they are similar challenges to those of teams working in the same physical space, only amplified by the constraints of virtual communication. For example, a team members' inability to see the body language of her colleague when she speaks may mean that she misses some highly important non-verbal cues, which makes a considerable, if subtle, difference to the meaning of her words. Furthermore, in some cultures the need to actually see the person with whom you are doing business is a crucial aspect of building a trusted business relationship. All of this can have a detrimental impact on team- and relationship-building, information-sharing, and so on - if not dealt with promptly and sensitively at an early stage of team formation.

Such difficulties can, of course, be overcome, with some small but important adjustments of communication practices and 'groundrules'. In the diagram below we give an overview of some of the key challenges faced by both traditional and virtual teams and also add some specifics for virtual teams .

As you can see from this overview, there is one type of challenge that repeats itself on the virtual team side of the diagram, and that is managing the impact of distance upon team members. In our experience, there are **FOUR DIFFERENT TYPES** of distance which can test the abilities of virtual teams and their leaders, and these are defined and described in more detail on the next pages.

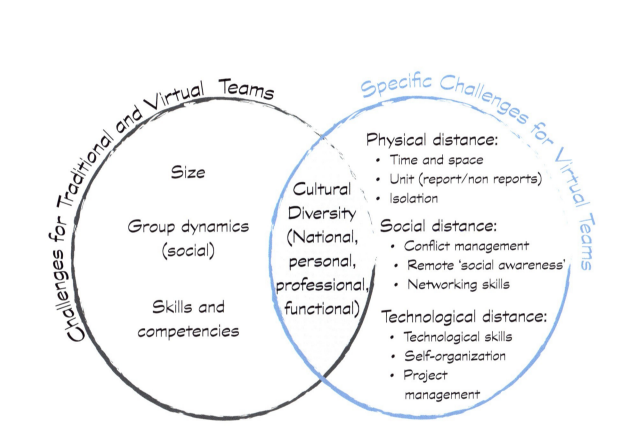

Fig. 2. Traditional Teams vs. Virtual Teams Challenges.© Doujak Corporate Development

CHAPTER 1 INTRODUCTION

Fig. 3. Four Types of Distance Affecting Virtual Teams © Doujak Corporate Development

Let's look at these four different types of distance in turn.

PHYSICAL DISTANCE is the most prominent and obvious, of course, referring **not only to spatial distance, where team members are geographically dispersed, but also taking into account the impact of different time zones and working hours**. These kind of differences bring challenges as well as benefits – they require a much closer attention to planning for any remote team leader, in order to simplify collaboration among team members across locations, countries and continents.

On the other hand, as commented above, being able to work on projects 24 hours a day by splitting the work geographically in order to take advantage of daylight in one part of the world (while team members are asleep in another) is a very considerable advantage.

Physical distance can sometimes exacerbate challenges which may be addressed more swiftly in teams operating face to face. One example of this is the 'matrix' reporting system typical in many large organisations these days, where team leaders may have employees in their teams who are not directly accountable to them. Managing employees who do not report to you directly may well require a different leadership style than that used with team members who do, and this point applies as much to co-located as to virtual teams.

Physical distance

OVERCOMING PHYSICAL DISTANCE:
- **MONITOR HIDDEN CONFLICTS**
- **MANAGE THE NEW "VIRTUAL REPORTING" SYSTEM**
- **SPLIT THE WORK GEOGRAPHICALLY FOR A 24H APPROACH**

However, there is a key difference. In virtual teams, the physical distance between personnel can sometimes mean that relationship building is neglected, and any latent, hidden conflicts might be more difficult to identify and address swiftly than in the face-to-face team setting. To this extent, physical distance among team members can sometimes also cause emotional distance and disengagement, if not well-managed. Misunderstandings can arise due to poor communication, and the challenge of getting immediate answers to tricky questions when the person who can answer them is asleep on the other side of the world, for example. Therefore it is crucial to establish a clear communication, and task, 'flow' where the status of certain deliverables is visible for everyone no matter at what time of the day. There are many online collaboration systems which can support this process but the main basis for it is that all team members agree and adjust to a joint working and communication style which requires time and trust building.

While conflict can be a stimulus for innovation as much as a hurdle to team progress, there is no doubt that virtual team leaders need to monitor the disputes and emotional disengagement that can arise when a team of very different people working across distance do not spend enough time getting to know and trust each other. Without this, a serious breakdown in collaboration may occur. With it, productive collaboration, mutual respect and understanding is far more likely. One key aspect to monitor and deal with hidden conflicts is to not only look at the

CHAPTER 1 INTRODUCTION

task related issues but also take social matters into account. There will be more information on the social matters in the next section "Managing relationships and tasks".

So much for the challenges of physical distance. What about **SOCIAL DISTANCE?** The phrase suggests **the difficulties associated with social interaction among remote teams or individual team members that are caused by diverse settings and lack of face to face contact.** In face-to-face teams, relationship building happens naturally through informal contact, spontaneous conversation on the way to the meeting room or around the coffee machine. These informal chats can sometimes be about personal matters, fostering greater trust and building relationships, or they might be more formal, discussing and sharing views on work topics, current organisational issues and so on. This kind of easy, unforced interaction is far more than just a pleasant form of social engagement. It is a key source of knowledge-sharing in any organisation, and one which is notoriously difficult to replicate in the virtual environment.

Social distance is probably the least obvious factor in any discussion of virtual team challenges, but it exerts, nevertheless, a considerable impact on the team's performance. Why? One big challenge for virtual team leaders and team members is the danger of isolation, a feeling of being cut-off from social and professional interaction with colleagues which can be extremely demotivating and draining of energy and confidence at times. The good news is that the challenges of 'social distance' can be overcome. There are some concrete and easily applicable interventions that can be used to prevent them, including a commonly-used technique of creating a 'virtual café' space at the start of a meeting, or an 'intranet chat room' where informal talk can take place.

A 'virtual café' is an online space where people meet on a regular basis e.g. every Friday from 9pm to 10pm to chat, exchange both work-related, but also private, information, everything that they would usually talk about at the coffee bar in the cafeteria or in the office kitchen. This can also be applied half an hour before a 'fixed' meeting to enable people to connect again and have a smooth start into the meeting. The 'intranet chat room' could be an online space where people can post questions or comments and get support by other team colleagues who are online. This could replace the usual face to face – over the table - conversation where you ask your colleague sitting next to you "what do you think of this graph? Is it self-explanatory?..." Instead of leaning over to your colleague's table, you post the question and the graph on a site and get an instant 'sounding board' and feedback from your peers.

Social distance

Overcoming social distance:
- *Foster informal chats*
- *Create interaction to avoid the feeling of isolation*
- *Give people a "face" (picture or video)*

CULTURAL DISTANCE refers to multiple **differences, not just of national culture, but also of corporate, professional and personal cultures, and the language differences that exist within these distinct cultures.** Managing these differences is already a challenge in multinational teams who are able to meet face-to-face, and predictably the challenge is exacerbated when working and communicating virtually.

There are several reasons for this. For a start, working 'styles' and expectations regarding what is acceptable may vary across culture, such as giving feedback (whether it is usual to do this via a direct or via an indirect style, for example), expectations about time and deadlines (how punctual and timely individuals and teams are expected to be), and whether or not any particular culture favours a more structured or a more flexible way of accomplishing tasks. Furthermore, there may also be a difference on the level of working processes and practices which vary between regions, and these should be spelled out at the beginning of a virtual team's formation.

Again, these potential difficulties are not impossible to overcome. A key point is that it is really necessary to invest time in knowing the social and working habits and expectations of team members from different cultures, and to take the time and effort to understand, and correctly interpret, differences in communication styles, according to both cultural and individual

CHAPTER 1 INTRODUCTION

Cultural distance

Overcoming cultural distance:
- *Provide intercultural coaching & training*
- *Share local practices*
- *Clarify and exchange views right from the beginning*

preferences. Possible solutions in overcoming cultural distance are intercultural trainings/ coaching but also clarifications and exchange of views right from the beginning.

TECHNOLOGICAL DISTANCE refers to the **role that technology plays in creating a sense of distance in virtual teams, while at the same time having the potential of bringing people together.** Therefore technical tools for communication have a significant impact on interactions between individuals and also at team level. Virtual communication has a vast array of tools which can certainly be of assistance in building a virtual team, including email, intranet, internet, VOIP, instant messaging, blogs, wikis, web-seminars, podcasts, webcasts, video conferences and telephone conferences. If these tools are used inappropriately, however, they can and often do prevent rather than support the development of collaboration, communication and a trusting environment in any virtual team.

Other problems which can be created when technology reinforces rather than minimises the challenge of distance relate to the tendency of some virtual team leaders to neglect to spend time building relationships and trust between team members. Unfortunately, this oversight frequently means information-sharing is limited, and the team's performance is usually lower as a result. Other problems that occur when technology hinders open communication in a virtual team include ongoing power struggles between members that may drain confidence and morale, as well as 'communication breakdowns' relating to unresolved conflict. It's not hard to see how all of this can have a highly detrimental effect upon a virtual team's effectiveness and productivity.

Technological distance

OVERCOMING TECHNOLOGICAL DISTANCE:

- *TRAIN PEOPLE FROM THE START ON VIRTUAL TECHNOLOGIES*
- *USE AND PROVIDE THE RIGHT TOOL FOR THE RIGHT PURPOSE*
- *CHALLENGE PEOPLE'S MINDSET ON WORKING WITH A NEW SYSTEM*

However, there is hope: using the right tools for the right purpose definitely can help stimulate relationship building, thereby leading to a higher level of trust in virtual teams and a higher level of team performance overall. We have found that teams who are open in their attitudes to learning about virtual tools, and who are ready to receive training on which tools to use for which purpose, are usually more effective in communicating effectively. In general, a 'best practice' handbook can be an invaluable source of detailed information for virtual teams, covering topics such as how to best match the appropriate technology to the required task, the richness of data or level of information required in accomplishing the task , and the subsequent tools which are best suited to this task. Further on in this book, we provide a more detailed description of the use of technology and how to choose the right media.

TRAINING AND PREPARATION is an important step towards the easier adoption of virtual working as some of the possible challenges people may face can be overcome beforehand. Furthermore queries about using virtual tools can be answered at the training stage, and any fears or concerns can be raised and dealt with early on. It's also worth remembering, when considering ways of managing 'technological distance', that many communication challenges can be overcome when team members can have 'visual contact'. Meaning that the ability to see a face, be it a photo or a live video image, helps enormously in building up trust and getting crucial hints on the mood of the other person and how he/she might feel about any topic under discussion.

CHAPTER 1 INTRODUCTION

1.4. MANAGING RELATIONSHIPS AND TASKS – WHAT VIRTUAL TEAM LEADERS NEED TO KNOW

> *To develop high performing virtual teams it is necessary to focus on the relationship as much as on the task.*[5]
>
> Ghislaine Caulat

[5] Caulat G., (2010) Virtual Leadership: Rethinking Virtual Teams.

In the above section we have focussed on four types of distance that have an impact when working virtually, each bringing with them specific kinds of challenges. We have also suggested some general solutions which we hope you will find helpful. To end this part of the book, we want to look now at the most common theme of all in working virtually – managing relationships as well as tasks – and to explore how this topic affects individuals, teams and organisations. We also want to suggest ways in which you can manage it effectively.

Ghislaine Caulat[3], Head of the Virtual Working Practice Group at Ashridge Management College in the UK, emphasizes this aspect (2010): "To develop high performing virtual teams it is necessary to focus on the relationship as much as on the task".

The reality is that one of the most common mistakes that virtual teams make is to ignore this crucial aspect of social dynamics and connection among team members. In our diagram on the next page you can see key aspects relating to managing tasks (the left-hand column) and those relating to managing the social dynamics of virtual team interaction (right-hand column). You can also see how they affect individuals, teams, and organisations, as shown by the lateral/horizontal dimensions. Needless to say, all of these aspects are important and must be kept in mind and managed within the team on a continuous basis.

CHAPTER 1 INTRODUCTION

	TASKS	**SOCIAL**
INDIVIDUAL	• Managing the technology • Managing time shifts • Managing the personal work • Dealing with Information overload	• New leadership skills on virtual collaboration • New skills of team members on virtual collaboration • Independent working style – skills in managing oneself
TEAM 	• Showing/achieving results • Decision- making • Communication and information flow • Coordination of tasks and work flow • Learning together	• Building trust and relationships • Social networking • Actively planning social time • Detecting hidden conflicts • Managing conflict
ORGANISATION 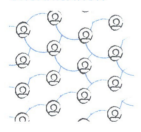	• Developing a blueprint to support virtual collaboration • Managing virtual teams • Providing access to technology and training	• Provide solutions to overcome isolation of virtual team members • Create a sense of loyalty and belonging • Deal with complex virtual structures

Fig. 4: Aspects of Remote Leadership Virtual Team Leaders Should Consider When Managing Task and Relationship-Related Challenges. © Doujak Corporate Development

FOR INDIVIDUAL TEAM MEMBERS, task-related challenges vary from managing the communications technology available to managing information flow, balancing workloads, and coping with time differences. On a social level, issues for individuals revolve around acquiring 'new' leadership skills which differ crucially from those applicable in the face to face setting. These may include efficiency in 'steering' virtual projects towards completion across distance, motivating people virtually, controlling workloads/workflow and being able to solve conflict. We will address this topic more in Chapter 3. Individual challenges are largely based around the training and preparation for leading in the virtual world, and around self-management - very important skills to be a successful collaborator in the virtual world.

On a **TEAM LEVEL**, challenging tasks include achieving results and putting into practice the training that individual members have received. This is likely to require excellent communication, a transparent decision-making process, and open discussions which help team members to coordinate their work and create the kind of learning environment that supports innovation. On a social level it's about building trust in relationships, dealing with the lack of face-to-face contact by actively planning social time, as well as dealing with conflicts which will likely occur and may affect performance of the team in general if not solved properly.

So much for balancing the task fulfilment and the relationship-building aspects of virtual teamwork at individual and team level. We consider it very important to think about how to do this **ACROSS THE WHOLE ORGANISATION**, and one of the biggest challenges here is that many organisations lack the required knowledge to establish and support virtual teams. This is particularly relevant when you consider the high risk of individual isolation when working virtually, leading often to a sense of detachment from the organisation which can lead to a general mistrust in organisational processes and purposes, but more seriously perhaps a complete disengagement over time. When the signs of individual isolation are not recognised and managed properly early on, the cost is consequently high in talent retention terms later.
Often significant demotivation results, ultimately causing resignation and departure of highly valued and experienced personnel.

Creating an environment or culture within the organisation that supports virtual interaction is not, therefore, simply about 'forcing' employees to use virtual technology but rather making it available and technologically accessible/understandable for everybody. More important still, it is about presenting the arrival of virtual working as an enjoyable opportunity rather than merely a time-consuming requirement.

CHAPTER 1 INTRODUCTION

ARE VIRTUAL TEAMS A MAGIC RECIPE FOR EVERYTHING?

While it is true that virtual teams will likely become the "norm" in the future, arguing that they will completely replace traditional teams finally is perhaps rather a strong statement. However it seems probable that a combination of "blended" virtual and face-to-face working (such as when organising regular team get-togethers) will remain a preference, when it is achievable.

And it is worth remembering that there are some key situations where virtual teams may not be the best choice – or can be more challenging. They include the following:

- Where there are too many contributors required to collaborate in one complete team.
- Where face to face interaction is required on a constant basis – for example, where highly scientific procedures are required.
- Where fears remain about the reliability of the technology, even when it has been extensively used. Mistrusting the software can seriously hinder a team's progress.
- Where there is no record of successful previous collaboration from the team participants and their department. Teams that have failed in face to face collaboration might need to work out unresolved issues which have not yet come fully to light before they head over to a 'virtual approach'. Otherwise the conflicts might continue virtually, but remain hidden and thus potentially more damaging in the longer term.
- Where there is inadequate resources to support the kind of team building process required for a virtual team to succeed.

Nevertheless we are convinced that virtual working is a powerful new standard for collaboration. It is up to the individual team leader and team member to contribute and make the team successful - but it is also the organisation's responsibility to provide the right cultural and technological environment to make virtual working real.

In the next chapter we will deep dive into the "culture distance" we mentioned earlier, reflecting on the implications of culture in virtual teams and analyse some particular aspects that have a greater impact in the virtual setting.

CHAPTER 2 THE IMPLICATIONS OF CULTURE IN CROSS-CULTURAL VIRTUAL TEAMS

> *It is quite possible, even common, to work across cultures for decades and travel frequently for business while remaining unaware and uninformed about how culture impacts you. Millions of people work in global settings while viewing everything from their own culture perspective and assuming that all differences, controversy, and misunderstanding are rooted in personality. Many well-intentioned people don't educate themselves about cultural differences because they believe that if they focus on individual differences that will be enough.*
>
> Erin Meyer, "The Culture Map", 2014

2.1. WHY IS CULTURE IMPORTANT?

We notice that, following Erin Meyer's comment (2014), there has been an increasing tendency to believe that cultural differences are becoming less important in our globalised world because we are now more commonly used to working together with people, teams and companies from other cultures and cultural backgrounds. Additionally, there is a view that cultural differences in general matter less because globalisation itself has somehow broken down those 'barriers' and distinctions that existed before – the world, so to say, is somehow 'flatter' from a cultural perspective, and cultural differences are therefore easier to navigate.

Alongside this, corporate centralisation programs, whereby 'company HQ' tends to be focused in one single location with a singular corporate 'culture' emanating from it, is a parallel tendency that seeks to minimise the impact of cultural differences between regions in order to find a simpler way of running companies within the global complexity.

When you combine these factors with the advent of 'virtualization' in individual and team communication, with all the effort and focus that is required to overcome the challenges of geographical and other types of distance (see previous Chapter - Four types of distance influencing virtual teams) it is not hard to see how the concept of cultural distinction has become, one might say, somewhat 'side-lined' in the face of these trends.

From today's standpoint, it is undoubtedly true that for any individual, team or company, the fact of operating in a globalised world has made a very significant difference to how we see ourselves professionally, and what we need from others in the globalised business environment. However, the approach adopted by some multi-national corporations of trying to impose a singular strategy (and corporate culture) that will take shape in the same way and be universally appropriate in all regions and cultures within the global business has, in very many cases, proved to be unsuccessful.

The reasons for this are a combination of factors. Partly the lack of success has resulted from strategic decisions that do not "fit well' with the local reality because of different needs or focus, and partly because this kind of 'centralised' corporate culture sometimes triggers a sense of loss of local freedom and a feeling of being "controlled" by the Headquarters.

However, we can observe, in just the last few years, a reverse trend to the above. In other words, a gradual return to the idea of local and regional differences as valuable and worth honouring, a reintroduction of country managers rather than a fully-centralised leadership structure, and, in general, a more culturally-sensitive approach in major businesses across the world.

CHAPTER 2 THE IMPLICATIONS OF CULTURE IN CROSS-CULTURAL VIRTUAL TEAMS

So what does all this mean, in intercultural terms, for remote teams and their leaders in today's globally-dispersed world, where suppliers, research and development facilities, finance departments and headquarters are spread in multiple locations globally? It means several things, in fact. Firstly, that 'cross-cultural awareness' becomes vital. In Neeley's terms (2014): "People struggle with global teamwork, even though it is essential to success in multinational firms. Despite their efforts to nimbly manage differences in time zones, cultures, and languages, cross-border collaborators often fail to reach shared understanding or common ground. They face conflicting group norms, practices, and expectations — all of which can cause severe fracturing along cultural lines"[6].

In other words, being "cross-cultural aware" doesn't mean only knowing that there are cultural differences, but going more in-depth in understanding why people do things differently from you, explaining to others how you see the world, how YOUR culture influences your behaviour, and finally — and most important of all - learning from each other. Secondly, it means that a 'new' kind of leader is required, one with the kind of intercultural competence and awareness suggested here, and the ability to adapt smoothly to widely diverse ways of working, communicating and evaluating team and individual performance and progress. Thirdly, it demands of the leader that his/her learning must be dynamic, continuous and evolutionary — constantly adapting and adjusting to the multiple and changing needs of the cultural context and requirements within which s/he operates.

If you 'google' the question "What is culture?" you will come across about 1,450,000,000 search results.[7] There has been, and continues to be, an extraordinary amount of time and effort spent attempting to define and "visualise" what the term 'culture' really means. These attempts have led to a variety of both well-known and lesser-known theoretical models, one of the former being the "iceberg model"[8], a key point of which is that what really matters about culture, like values and beliefs, is below the water and thus invisible.

In other words, what we understand about culture, or are able to detect in cross-cultural communications, is only the "tip of the iceberg", compared to the hidden nuances and subtle distinctions that lie concealed underneath the water's surface, according to this metaphor. This idea of culture as a concept with both an obvious, detectable impression or visibility, and hidden roots and influences is a common theme, and in another visual representation or model culture thus appears as a tree.

6 Neeley T., "Getting Cross-Cultural Teamwork Right, Harvard Business Review, 2015
7 Google search "What is Culture?": 1,450,000,000 search results on 12.10.2015
8 Image Iceberg Model: http://www.differencedifferently.edu.au/defining_identities/part_1a.php 4

Arts
Language
Behaviours
Dress   Foods
Celebrations

Values   Customs   Roles

Traditions

Beliefs

Rules   Status

Tought patterns   Perceptions

CHAPTER 2 THE IMPLICATIONS OF CULTURE IN CROSS-CULTURAL VIRTUAL TEAMS

The notion of culture as not only rooted in, and emerging from multiple contexts, but also as a kind of all-important, life-enhancing environment whose impact we take for granted until it is absent is described elsewhere as similar to the idea of taking a fish out of water.
As Kai Hammerich and Richard Lewis (2013)[9] point out in their book, a fish realises the need for water only when water is not around anymore, as it is something natural for it, taken for granted. Our own culture is like water to a fish. We live and "swim" through it. When you ask somebody who has spent his whole life in the same city to describe his own culture, he might find it hard and might end up saying "we don't really have a culture here".

It seems that we need to be aware that the impact of culture is indeed universal. **We are all influenced by culture, whatever version of culture this may mean – national, regional, corporate or professional.**

In order to explore this impact, and the distinctions between different kinds of culture, we have developed the **"Individual Culture Model"** ©.

As you'll see in the following diagram, the concept of culture is shown as going beyond national cultures and deriving from a combination of different cultural influences. The individual is placed in the middle, and the intent of the model is not only to show how many different cultures co-exist, but also that they are all interrelated and influence each person's "Individual Culture". Therefore **we can define the Individual Culture as the special combination of cultural traits** deriving from your national culture(s), the corporate culture of the organisation you are currently working in (or have worked in previously for a relevant amount of time), your professional culture (you would agree if we say that the 'IT culture' is quite different from that of HR or Marketing), and your personal culture (that includes your age, personality and any relevant experiences).

The four different cultures identified in this model are thus national culture, corporate culture, professional culture and personal culture. The definition of each culture emerges from and relates to the following questions:

---

9 Hammerich K., Lewis R., "Fish Can't See Water: How National Cultures Can Make or Break Your Corporate Strategy", Wiley, 2013

- Where are you from?
- Where do your parents come from?
- Where did you grow up?
- Which culture has the most impact on you (national, regional, city culture)?
- Which characteristics of your national culture influence the way you are?

- What subject/s did you study?
- What are your most important work experiences?
- What is your current function and job title?
- How would you describe the "working approach" and values within your profession?

- What are the key characteristics of your organisational culture (local unit/HQ unit)?
- What are your organisation's values and principles?
- How would you describe the 'common working style'?
- What are the main differences/similarities within the organisational culture, when you compare HQ with local units?

- How would your best friend describe your personality?
- Do you consider yourself as being more introvert or extravert?
- Do you consider yourself as being more task-oriented or relationship-oriented?
- What would you say were the life-changing events that continue to have an influence within your 'personal culture'?

Fig. 5: Individual Culture Model. © Elisa Alberto

CHAPTER 2 THE IMPLICATIONS OF CULTURE IN CROSS-CULTURAL VIRTUAL TEAMS

The model you see here evolved following a memorable conversation with an experienced intercultural trainer we know. He once said to us, with some concern on his face:

"There's something bothering me about culture. If, after having worked so long in this field, I still regularly fall into cross-cultural misunderstandings - how could I possibly claim that somebody with no intercultural knowledge would get any lasting benefit from a one-day intercultural training?".

It was an excellent reminder of a missing ingredient in existing cultural theories and dimensions, which, although they offer useful tools and give us a framework for understanding culture, make little reference to individual differences. From this point on, we started thinking about a different approach that would move the focus from the idea of culture in general to the unique individual needs and distinctions that will exist within that very broadly defined term.

Why? It became clear to us that simply knowing about cultural theories and models is not enough, because this knowledge loses its purpose if we do not understand first who we are as individuals and how we behave. For example – it may not help much to know that Germans have a more direct communication style if we don't know first that we ourselves are quite indirect in comparison. When using this model which places the individual at its heart, **people are obliged to reflect on who they are, and how those different cultural influences acting upon them make a difference to the way they uniquely think, act and view other people.**

From this focus on the individual at the centre of cultural difference, a number of important themes emerge. The first one is the recognition that, in dealing successfully and skilfully with people from other cultures it is crucial to have a clear understanding of your own culture.

You might consider your national culture (red circle in the model) to be Austrian, as you were born in Vienna and raised in Salzburg and your parents are also both Austrian. You have now been working in Germany for 10 years for an automotive company at the HQ, in which case the corporate culture of the company (grey circle in the model) as well as the local national culture (again red circle) have almost certainly also influenced your 'Individual Culture'. Let's also imagine that you are working in IT, which is what you have studied and the field you have been working in for many years. Being an IT expert is therefore most likely to determine your "professional culture" (blue circle in the model). Last but not least, as each individual regardless of any other cultural influences will also have his own unique personality, you may say that others describe you as being very task-oriented and rather introverted (green circle). What is important to note here is that this may stand out in contrast to the traits from other cultures (like being Brazilian but being always 100% on time, which is not the general trait in Brazil) and even more important his or her own personal history and life experiences, which are absolutely unique.

HERE'S AN EXAMPLE.

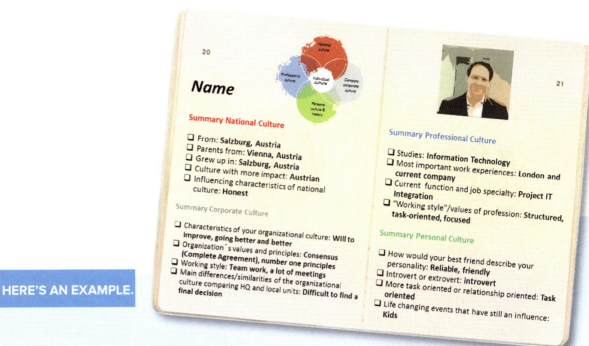

Fig. 6: "Passport" visualization of the culture model

The **"passport visualization"** is a simplification of the example we just described according to the four cultures. **To summarize, the combination of the 4 cultures (national, corporate, professional and personal) creates that special "mix" of cultural influences that is UNIQUE for each individual - and this is exactly what your "Individual Culture" means - at the core of the model.**

We therefore find that using this model as a self-reflection or team development tool really helps in breaking down the complex nature of the idea of culture and serves to divert us effectively from easy cultural stereotypes, drawing our attention back to individual divergence and uniqueness. And, at the same time, we also have to remember that culture is emergent, changing all the time. This is particularly true when we look at individual culture. If you have spent, as we have, about one third of your life in a more "direct" culture, you will of course find it has influenced the way you communicate, which may be rather different from your communication style before exposure to that direct cultural approach.

CHAPTER 2 THE IMPLICATIONS OF CULTURE IN CROSS-CULTURAL VIRTUAL TEAMS

Finally, culture is also something that we view subjectively: the way we look at one culture can be totally different from the way somebody else looks at the same culture. Of course this is at least partly because the lens through which each of us sees the world is different from someone else's cultural lens, shaped by our own experiences and life history. So the danger that we need to avoid here is that of oversimplifying cultural differences, or to consider that we have somehow become expert in what any particular culture is like. As Erin Meyer (2014) mentions, "If an executive wants to build and manage global teams that can work together successfully, he needs to understand not just how people from his own culture experience people from various international cultures, but also how those international cultures perceive one another"[10].

To conclude, one of my favourite quotes:

> *Seeing is not believing; believing is seeing! You see things, not as they are, but as you are.*
>
> Eric Butterworth

10 Meyer E., "One Reason Cross-Cultural Small Talk Is So Tricky", Harvard Business Review, 2014, p 23

2.2. INTERCULTURAL DIFFERENCES THAT HAVE AN IMPACT IN VIRTUAL TEAMS

During the survey that Doujak Corporate Development conducted on virtual teams in 2012[11], the challenge of working across cultures came across from several interviews. A strategy that we find very useful when navigating the complexity of culture, most particularly in a virtual setting, is to focus on tangible business situations instead of talking generally about cultural traits. For example, instead of talking about cultures being 'direct' or "indirect" in their communication style, we prefer to look at a specific situation – such as giving and receiving feedback – and how the cultural characteristic under discussion impacts upon that particular work situation.

11 Report "Leading International Virtual Teams: Challenges and best practices of virtual teams", Viviana Rojas de Amon, 2012

CHAPTER 2 THE IMPLICATIONS OF CULTURE IN CROSS-CULTURAL VIRTUAL TEAMS

The "classic" cultural dimensions, those well-known ones defined by Hofstede (1991) or Trompenaars and Hampden-Turner (1997), have been a great framework for navigating the complexity of culture but are not necessarily proving to be relevant in virtual space. Instead, other dimensions seem to have become more important and, if disregarded, could cause significant challenges in the virtual setting. They include:

- Communication, 'small talk' and 'conversational turn-taking' in different cultures
- Giving (critical) feedback in an intercultural virtual environment
- Different perceptions of the importance of time and 'timeliness' across culture and space
- Building relationships and trust across cultures and distance

Taking these in the order shown above, here are some specific challenges, and ideas about how to handle these in virtual teams.

COMMUNICATION: WHEN IS IT TIME TO TALK AND TIME TO BE SILENT?

" The most important thing in communication is hearing what isn't said.

Peter Drucker

CHAPTER 2 THE IMPLICATIONS OF CULTURE IN CROSS-CULTURAL VIRTUAL TEAMS

COMMUNICATION: WHEN IS IT TIME TO TALK AND TIME TO BE SILENT?

Communication surely plays a very important role in virtual interactions, and the biggest challenge is probably caused by the lack of face-to-face communication. The danger here is to believe that the definition of "effective communication" is the same in every culture - a belief which can often cause misunderstandings and tension within the team.

A practical example of this is the way **'small talk'** is done, something which differs very much across cultures, not only in terms of what people will talk about to get to know each other and build rapport initially and how people engage in 'small talk', but also about the meaning of it and its business implications in different cultures. As Andy Molinsky points out, "In many cultures — especially those with more formal rules for communication and with a strong emphasis on social hierarchy — it's considered inappropriate to engage in casual conversation with superiors. In addition, it can also feel impolite and even dangerous to openly express your opinion during small talk, especially if it could potentially conflict with the other person's opinion"[12].

In a virtual environment, engaging in 'small talk' can be even harder than in the face to face setting. Building up social contact virtually is already quite challenging, and knowing what is appropriate in your "colleague's world" could surely help in building up the right basis for the communication.

A key consideration in this is that **the appropriateness of sharing personal information with somebody we do not know well varies significantly from country to country.**
It is, for example, generally wrong to assume that the more relationship-oriented a culture is, the more small talk is likely to be important in that culture, and personal in nature.
In fact, it is very often the other way around, and one reason for that is probably that small talk has different purposes in different cultures.

Taking the examples of the US and Germany, Americans are generally well-known for starting friendly and personal conversations with strangers, which some people might interpret as being very relationship-focused. In the US culture it is necessary to engage in small talk in order for people to feel they can trust each other and also to show your colleagues you are a trustful person. But **how do you cope with it when two cultures with totally different "rules" for small talk are obliged to build a relationship in virtual space?**

---

12 Molinsky A., "The Big Challenge of American Small Talk", Harvard Business Review, 2013

In the German culture, for example, being "forced" into small talk might be entirely counter-productive in a relationship-building context, as establishing a personal relationship at work in Germany is something that takes rather longer than the time required for a few short, friendly conversations.

The main question then is probably: **WHEN is it appropriate to talk about non-work related topics or to ask personal questions?** Erin Meyer summarizes what happens when we ignore this important question very clearly in a recent HBR article "It was my first dinner party in France and I was chatting with a Parisian couple. All was well until I asked what I thought was a perfectly innocent question: 'How did the two of you meet?' My husband Eric (who is French) shot me a look of horror. When we got home he explained:
'We don't ask that type of question to strangers in France. It's like asking them the colour of their underpants'."[13]

We believe the best way to deal with these differences is, first of all, to know your communications preferences (and expectations) and then try to agree on an approach that helps you in building a relationship but leaves you still feeling comfortable within it. If small talk is for you a way of building relationships, you might also consider having more "in-depth" phone conversations to build up trust and strengthen your (virtual) relationships or to avoid asking too many personal questions of others at the beginning of a new relationship, even if you feel quite willing to share personal information about yourself freely. If you are from a culture that appreciates a rather longer time span to build up deep relationships, try not to misunderstand others' behaviour as being somehow inauthentic when they do not seem to share your preferences - but rather as their way of communicating and building relationships, which is different from yours.

13 E. Meyer, "One Reason Cross-Cultural Small Talk Is So Tricky", Harvard Business Review, 2014

CHAPTER 2 THE IMPLICATIONS OF CULTURE IN CROSS-CULTURAL VIRTUAL TEAMS

Another interesting aspect of communication is **turn-taking**, how we signal to others that it is their turn to speak or that we are about to finish speaking and give someone else the floor. Most people have their own approach to this, and there are major differences in whether overlapping with someone else ('interrupting' unintentionally, or speaking over them) is acceptable or not in a conversation, whether silence between conversations is acceptable, and which signs we should give in order to signal that someone else can now speak.

Quite aside from this, the question of what is acceptable in terms of the length of a conversation can be very different from culture to culture. Germans, for example, tend to speak longer before handing over to another person than English speakers do. Similarly, people from cultures which appreciate some "breaks" in-between conversations may be overwhelmed by a culture that is uncomfortable with silence. When talking about having conference calls with colleagues in the US, a Swedish colleague once told me: "It is hard to react and join the conversation as it seems they have to fill in every second of the call. To me it seems that they actually think while they talk, but here in Sweden we first think and then talk!"

EXAMPLES OF DIFFERENT TURN-TAKING:

Culture A: clear-cut distinction (or 1-2 seconds break) between conversations (no overlap) → Eg: Germany

Culture B: overlapping between conversations → Eg: Italy

CHAPTER 2 THE IMPLICATIONS OF CULTURE IN CROSS-CULTURAL VIRTUAL TEAMS

Going back to the metaphor of culture being like the water you "swim" in, **turn-taking patterns are hard to recognize at first – it will take time to become aware of them, whether/how they vary from your own, and to adjust to the different approach.** When living in Denmark I became quickly aware that my Italian turn-taking "style" was very tiring and not very effective in having a good conversation, as people were waiting until I would let them speak.
After going back home for a holiday I realized that the "Danish way" had already influenced me – or rather I had adapted in order to have meaningful conversations. One example of this came up one evening when discussing with some friends about where to have dinner. I found I had a hard time in choosing the right time to speak up and share my idea. In that moment I understood how my Danish colleague might have felt when talking to me during my first weeks in the office!

The **use of silence** can also differ considerably from one culture to another, especially between western and eastern cultures. For example, in some **eastern countries**, like Japan or India, silence often has a positive meaning, and is taken as a sign of depth, appreciation and credibility. According to these traditions, words can 'contaminate' an experience and the belief that inner peace and wisdom come only though silence. In order to keep harmony and maintain good relationships with others, eastern people often share their opinions only after thinking deeply, and silence is often used to express agreement.

In clear contrast to this, people from **western countries** like USA, Germany, and France see a silent reaction to a proposal or presentation as a negative response in international business communication. So keeping silent often during conversations with business people in eastern countries may sometimes be misunderstood, and misinterpreted as a lack of interest or, worse, an indication of a negative response to what is being discussed.

But you do not have to work with people as far afield as Japan to encounter differences in the meaning of silence and whether or not people feel comfortable with it. I remember talking to a Finnish friend on one occasion, and noticing that my perception was that she was a bit shy about expressing her opinion. As a result, I was aware that I was trying to fill in all the "silence breaks" during our conversation. Later on, I realised my mistake when I came across an article about **Finland** and discover that Finns do not appreciate engaged small-talks and see silence as an active part of the communication.

Taking these differences into the virtual setting, it is not hard to see how variations in how silence is used (and appreciated, or not) could become a challenge. Therefore, before coming to a quick conclusion about the "level of engagement" **in a virtual conversation, you may reflect on whether the meaning of silence could be different between you and your counterpart.**

When facilitating a webinar with an international audience, you usually can observe this particular distinction in the way people interact in the session. If you are doing a webinar with an Asian audience, say, you might expect less interaction than with an American audience. This is particularly relevant when the success of the webinar is determined by how interactive people were in the session (in terms of asking questions, speaking up and writing in the chat space). It's possible to see from this example how cultural differences may lead to misinterpretations if we are not aware of them. One way around this challenge is to be absolutely explicit about the 'rules' of communication for your session at the beginning. If you need people to be highly interactive and participative, you may want to say so clearly at the beginning, making sure that everybody knows how to do it and why - for instance, if you would like some feedback on your presentation.

CHAPTER 2 THE IMPLICATIONS OF CULTURE IN CROSS-CULTURAL VIRTUAL TEAMS

FEEDBACK: **TO WHAT EXTENT IS COMMUNICATING DIRECTLY 'CRITICAL FEEDBACK' ACCEPTABLE?**

> *Criticism may not be agreeable, but it is necessary. It fulfils the same function as pain in the human body. It calls attention to an unhealthy state of things.*
>
> Winston Churchill

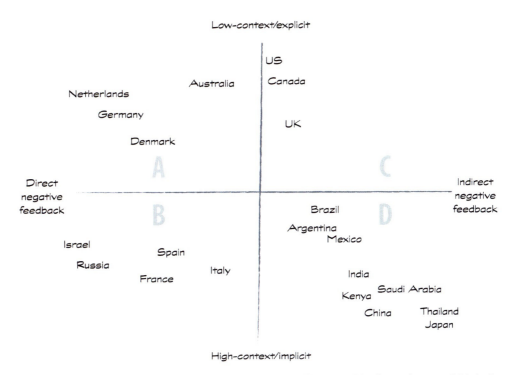

Fig. 7: Meyer E., "The Culture Map: Breaking Through The Invisible Boundaries of Global Business", Public Affairs, 2014 P. 72

The act of giving feedback to others is probably one of the most important kinds of interaction for any kind of team, whether virtual or face to face. Receiving positive feedback and being shown appreciation is something that everyone values, no matter which culture they come from. However, **giving negative feedback or criticism is of course a rather different matter. Apart from some common sense behaviours to be aware of, there is no universally-effective way of giving feedback.**

Coming across Erin Meyer's (2014) mapping of the 'communication scale' (relating to giving direct and indirect negative feedback with both a 'low-context' or 'high-context' communication approach) was for me an eye-opener in explaining such an important aspect. As defined by Edward Hall[14], low-context cultures communicate information in a direct manner that relies mainly on word and do not rely on contextual elements (i.e., the speaker's tone of voice or body language) to communicate information, while high-context cultures rely heavily on implicit messages and contextual cues (i.e., the situation and the speaker's tone of voice) to relay information being communicated.

For example, looking at Meyer's model (fig. 7), one idea we might have to discard is **that cultures which have a more direct and straightforward communication preference would automatically have a preference for direct negative feedback.** In Meyer's graph,

14 Hall E. T:, "Beyond Culture", 1976

CHAPTER 2 THE IMPLICATIONS OF CULTURE IN CROSS-CULTURAL VIRTUAL TEAMS

quadrants B and C look particularly interesting, because they list some cultures that one might expect to behave differently from what is suggested here.

An example: if you think about the US, you may assume that Americans are quite straightforward and clear in their communication style. Yet when looking at this particular dimension, the US falls more into the indirect side, as negative feedback is always nicely "wrapped" and introduced by positive feedback. Diagonally opposite to the US on this model, we notice France is listed in the cultures which fall within a more implicit/'high context' communication approach, yet also – as indicated here – prefer (and are used to) giving direct negative feedback.

An exercise we often use during teambuilding with culturally-diverse international audiences is to ask participants to position themselves on a scale with two extremes (see figure 8):

- We invite people to stand on the left side of the room if they prefer to give (and receive) **negative feedback in a direct and honest way**, liking to be transparent and not "soften" their message with indirect behaviour or "package" it with positive feedback.

- We invite people to stand on the right side of the room if they prefer to give (and receive) **negative feedback in a softer way**, avoiding straightforward feedback, and giving criticism only in private.

Once people have positioned themselves appropriately, we go around, moving from one extreme of the scale to the other, and asking people what their preference is and why. Very often during this activity, participants explain how in their country people give negative feedback, and what anyone doing so has to be careful about. What is therefore most useful in this exercise is for people to realize how different their team colleagues (or subordinates) may be in their approach when dealing with exactly the same business scenario.

"HOW DO YOU GIVE NEGATIVE FEEDBACK?"

Fig. 8: Scale Exercise "Preferences on Giving and Receiving Negative Feedback",
© Doujak Corporate Development.

TEAM DEVELOPMENT WITH AN INTERNATIONAL TEAM

I once facilitated a team of about 14 people with 10 different nationalities. They were facing some challenges in trust and collaboration, but believed that having worked together already over some time in Europe, most of them would be "Europeanised" in their way of working – in other words, acclimatised to similar rules and preferences that would be universally acceptable within the team. As it turned out, it was quite astonishing for them to see how different they actually were in their preferences, in terms of the scale activity above. The French leader positioned himself on the very left side (direct negative feedback) while the Indian and the Filipino leaders positioned themselves on the very right side (indirect feedback) explaining that, even though they adapted their behaviour when receiving feedback, when giving negative feedback they still preferred to communicate it very indirectly and 'in-between the lines'. This example shows how despite the "Europeanised" team and adaptations team members had made to fit around each other's preferences, still the cultural background of each individual continued to exert a deep impact on his or her communication style.

CHAPTER 2 THE IMPLICATIONS OF CULTURE IN CROSS-CULTURAL VIRTUAL TEAMS

As already mentioned, there is quite often a tendency among team members and leaders to believe that you are using a more "universally-acceptable" approach that should work in any context – or that your team has been working together for such a long time that you have implicitly developed a "common style" already. However, when dealing with a topic as sensitive as giving criticism, our deeper values and beliefs very often continue to influence the way we act and react to others, even when there are trusting and well-established business relationships involved. And of course, as discussed in the culture model presented in the first paragraph, we should not forget about the impact of individual personality differences in the 'culture equation' as well.

Translating these considerations into the virtual meeting space, we see challenges coming up for participants with preferences for either a direct, or an indirect communication style. For people coming from cultures that prefer and appreciate negative feedback to be given indirectly, it may be challenging to find a way to communicate it virtually, since a face to face situation may feel more private than a virtual scenario where you may, or may not, be able to see the face of the person you are speaking to.

When coming from a culture that actively prefers and appreciates direct negative feedback, you may find the virtual technology "effective" in conveying the message – but perhaps need to be aware that the message could come across as even more direct than in a face to face situation. When communicating directly face to face you may still use some other aspects of communication, such as body language, face expression or tone of voice to communicate some nuances about your message that do not come across in a written direct communication.

So, what exactly is the challenge here for the virtual team leader or member? Nothing less than this - to find the most appropriate way of giving feedback that not only suits the recipient of that feedback, but also allowing you to feel comfortable with your own style. This means, then, that a probable solution is not "going 100% local" (adapting your style 100% to the local culture and customs) but possibly also discovering and developing a style that avoids the extremes on the feedback scale above. It also suggests that clarifying with your counterpart what his/her preference is could be extremely useful.

Another illustration of this – you might find yourself in a situation where you are trying to adjust your own direct feedback style in order to fit around that of your Asian colleague, who you might assume prefers a more indirect approach to feedback. But this is not likely to be quite accurate, if that same Asian colleague has spent most of her life in Germany, say.
In this scenario, you may want to check beforehand what would be an effective working style for both of you – since it is possible that you may end up with similar preferences for the feedback conversation. "Managers in different parts of the world are conditioned to give feedback

in drastically different ways. The Chinese manager learns never to criticize a colleague openly or in front of others, while the Dutch manager learns always to be honest and to give the message straight. Americans are trained to wrap positive messages around negative ones, while the French are trained to criticize passionately and provide positive feedback sparingly" (Meyer, 2014)[15].

Another simple tip when giving feedback is also to learn about the **"communication channels"** that your colleagues may prefer. You might have a colleague who simply prefers e-mails to phone calls, and even though you may find it time-consuming and believe that a short phone call is more useful, it is worth making the effort necessary to find the right "tool" or channel for each team member.

WRONG INTERPRETATIONS ...

When I started working in Germany, I often felt offended at first by the way the client pointed out every single mistake I might have made and did not focus at all on what I'd done that was good. It took me some time to understand the deep value behind such behaviour, with its emphasis on efficiency and high quality by "saving" time that would otherwise have been spent talking about what is already good (so no need to spend time on it) and, instead, addressing straightaway the areas requiring improvement.

Elisa Alberto

15 Meyer E., "How To Say 'This Is Crap' In Different Cultures", Harvard Business Review, 2014

CHAPTER 2 THE IMPLICATIONS OF CULTURE IN CROSS-CULTURAL VIRTUAL TEAMS

Not being aware of the differences in communicating negative feedback could have major negative impact when dealing with what might be deemed "hidden messages" communicated in the working relationship. **If you come from a more direct culture, for example, you should develop skills to help you to interpret some "hidden" messages your less direct colleagues (or boss) might be communicating to you.** Erin Meyer's example is useful here:
"In Germany, we typically use strong words when complaining or criticizing in order to make sure the message registers clearly and honestly. Of course, we assume others will do the same. My British boss during a one-on-one "suggested that I think about" doing something differently. So I took his suggestion: I thought about it, and decided not to do it. Little did I know that his phrase was supposed to be interpreted as "change your behaviour right away or else." And I can tell you I was pretty surprised when my boss called me into his office to chew me out for insubordination!"

On the other side, if you come from a more indirect culture, which likes to focus on reading "between the lines" in communication, you may risk "interpreting" the message incorrectly, or simply "over-interpreting" a straightforward, direct message. One Japanese participant told me: **"I was having my early review with my Dutch boss and I was trying to read in between the lines about what he was saying. I could not believe he was talking about my mistakes so directly!"**

Therefore, one solution is to slightly adapt your style so that it suits your counterpart, but do not forget to keep your ears and eyes opened in interpreting (or not over-interpreting) what the other is saying.

TIME: HOW DO DIFFERENT PERCEPTIONS OF TIME AFFECT TEAM COLLABORATION WHEN WORKING VIRTUALLY?

> *The time is always right to do what is right.*
>
> Martin Luther King, Jr.

CHAPTER 2 THE IMPLICATIONS OF CULTURE IN CROSS-CULTURAL VIRTUAL TEAMS

COMMUNICATION: WHEN IS IT TIME TO TALK AND TIME TO BE SILENT?

Time is probably one of the cultural differences of which anyone who has ever dealt with people from other cultures will have some awareness or experience. And it is not simply a case of considering the time dimension in team collaboration as relating to being punctual, or late, by preference. The concept of time has other important nuances to consider when weighing up its impact on the team, such as being open to multi-tasking (or not) or whether you value more a focus on the immediate, short-term timescale, or the long-term perspective and outcomes.

Why is time such an important cultural difference when working virtually?
Here's a situation to consider. Let's imagine you are working with an international virtual team on a project and during the last virtual meeting you agreed on a project plan, distribution of tasks and deadlines. Now, the expectations on the next steps may vary quite widely across cultures. If you are German, you may expect that deadlines will be met, or at least that you will be informed about possible delays. An Italian, on the other hand, may find it acceptable to have some delay if this is for the purpose of finding a better solution. The German may follow the agreed process step by step, while the Italian may work on two tasks simultaneously if this brings her nearer to the desired outcome B.

In short, not only do the ways in which people work towards deadlines differ in diverse cultures; how to approach a process in order to get from A to B may also vary considerably.
Some cultures tend to prefer a more direct route following a clear, structured (and agreed) process, while other cultures allow some flexibility and may find an alternative way to reach B that changes the original plan. This is sometimes referred to (Richard Lewis[16]), in terms of having a "linear" or "monochromic" culture, or, conversely, a "flexible" or "polychromic" culture.

For example, cultures typically described as 'linear' – such as Switzerland, the Netherlands, Scandinavia and US – have a **linear vision of time and action**. They see time as something that is constantly passing, and that should not be wasted without decisions being made or actions being performed. Such cultures are usually also referred to as **monochromic**, in the sense that they prefer to do only one thing at a time, to concentrate on it and do it within a fixed schedule. On the other side, **'multi-active, flexible'** cultures such as those of Southern Europe or South American, are described as **polychromic** (doing several things at the same time), and are less interested in schedules and punctuality. Rather than accomplishing set tasks in an agreed order, for example, priority may instead be given to the relative thrill or significance of each meeting. The diagramme illustrates these key differences in sequencing and prioritising tasks over time.

---

[16] Lewis R., How Different Cultures Understand Time", Business Insider, 2014

Linear/Monochromic Culture:

Flexible/Polychromic Culture:

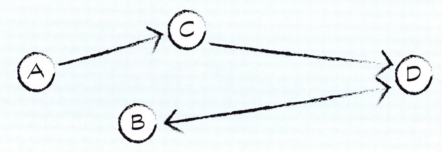

As this graphic indicates, people from "linear cultures" would typically not accept a change in the original action plan that has been discussed within the team, or the sequence of agreed tasks, while those from a flexible culture may not have any problem with changing the approach to task fulfilment as soon as the first key objective is reached.

If you are leading a multinational virtual team, you would do well to consider the differences among your team members regarding task-fulfilment and meeting deadlines. Failing to find an appropriate shared team culture about how to deal with tasks and deadlines can cause a great deal of frustration, not only for the leader but also for the whole team. It is important therefore to clarify everyone's expectations and preferences, to make sure everybody knows what is acceptable and what are 'no-go areas '.

And this is a good opportunity to clarify misconceptions. For example, Germans may be perceived in some cultures as being totally strict with deadlines; however, while dates are usually set to create a structured framework and clear steps to achieve the task, postponing of deadlines is still possible (it would mean creating a new plan with the new date).

CHAPTER 2 THE IMPLICATIONS OF CULTURE IN CROSS-CULTURAL VIRTUAL TEAMS

While task-fulfilment and meeting deadlines is important within the dimension of cultural differences relating to time – it is not the only aspect. The **dimension of punctuality** is one of the best known challenges, and can certainly weigh in as fairly significant in disrupting virtual collaboration, if ignored. Some cultures interpret being late to meetings as a sign of disrespect while other cultures which prioritize building relationships above getting on with the task can accept colleagues arriving late if the reason for lateness was that they were talking to somebody else!

Fogelberg and Tavanyar[17] give some good tips in their book on virtual facilitation, regarding how to deal with cultures where time is not managed in a linear way and relationship building is very important. Having a "Virtual Café" at the beginning of the meeting while waiting for the participants to join, is certainly a great idea to build relationships informally while waiting for any late participants, without this disturbing the group. They also emphasise the value of starting with a short "check-in process" (sharing something personal with the group) and a "check-out" at the end (short comment about a learning point, or 'take-away' from the meeting) is a good way to create a trusting atmosphere and provides a good "time frame" for all the participants.

Another element that varies considerably between cultures is in the scheduling and length of meetings. When I first started working in Germany, I realised how important it is to start and finish a meeting on time, as people may have another meeting starting exactly at the time your meeting ends. People from southern European cultures, for example, would probably not have such a "tight" schedule, and therefore would have more flexibility to accommodate a meeting running over time in their working day.

Here's another example of the challenges that arise from different cultural preferences about flexibility with time.

17 Fogelberg F., Tavanyar J., et al "Live connections: Virtual Facilitation for High Engagement and Powerful Learning", Nomadic, 2015, p. 166

Let's say you have organized a webinar with about 100 people in your organisation to present the new corporate values. You have planned one hour (45 minutes presentation + 15 minutes Q&A) overall and you also managed to start pretty much on time. So far, so good. But at the end of the meeting, during the Q&A session, you realise that time is up but there are still a lot of questions coming from your participants. What do you do? Here are some ideas. Firstly, you should consider your audience. Linear cultures (like Germany, Sweden or USA) value starting and finishing on time and also plan their time accordingly, therefore prolonging the meeting by 15 minutes may cause some problems in their schedule and some of your participants would therefore interpret this flexibility as "having badly managed the time". If you are working with a culturally-mixed audience, the best solution would be to announce that the official time of the meeting is over but that you are happy to answer further questions for anyone who can stay longer, or you can collect your questions and answer them "off-line" or in another meeting.

Scheduling meetings weeks or months in advance can also be challenging when working with other cultures. If you are a Danish manager, you may want to schedule your team meetings months in advance to have a clear "annual view" of what is coming up, while your Chinese counterparts would appreciate a more flexible schedule and would be ready to join a spontaneous meeting decided just a few hours before. To make sure that those long-term scheduled meetings are taken into consideration, it is necessary to contact the people concerned shortly beforehand, to make sure the meeting is still on their priority list (and that no other last-minute urgent matter has become more important).

CHAPTER 2 THE IMPLICATIONS OF CULTURE IN CROSS-CULTURAL VIRTUAL TEAMS

RELATIONSHIPS: WHAT IS NEEDED TO BUILD AND MAINTAIN TRUST?

> *A RELATIONSHIP WITHOUT TRUST IS LIKE A CAR WITHOUT GAS, YOU CAN STAY IN IT AS LONG AS YOU WANT BUT IT WON'T GO ANYWHERE.*
>
> Unknown

When building any kind of relationship, trust is probably the most important aspect. As mentioned in Forbes, "Trust helps us to manage the risks encountered when navigating everyday life"[18]. In other words, without trust you would need much more time to get everything done, and would also need to be an expert on everything. For example, imagine going to the doctor – any doctor – and not trusting her? Without trust, you would need to become your own doctor! Trust is not only a biological instinct that enables us to predict a positive outcome, but it is usually influenced by different experiences.

But **what do you need to trust somebody?**
I like to ask this question, when facilitating an international team workshop and I am always amazed to see how many different answers you actually get. For some people, trust is something that is influenced by the first impression they get of a person, while for others trust only develops during a long-term relationship. In a business environment trust could be the result of knowing that your colleague will deliver high-quality work on time, while for somebody else trust is built when you feel that a person is "there" for you, ready to step in if you need help.

TRUST IS A VITAL COMPONENT FOR SUCCESSFUL VIRTUAL TEAMS
It is a well-evidenced fact that no team can finally operate without trust, however defined.
As also defined by Greenberg et al. (2007) "Trust is critical to the cooperative behaviour that leads to the success of all teams, but it is especially important in virtual teams.
Two interrelated factors, diverse locations and technology-enabled communication, contribute to making trust more difficult to develop in virtual teams than in traditional hierarchical relationships and on-site teams"[19].

Without trust, in all its many senses, people may not share information freely, or they might battle over rights and responsibilities, or even not cooperate effectively with one another. Internal competition and politics may become an issue and no matter how talented your people are, they may never reach their full potential if trust is not present.

It follows from this that leaders of distributed virtual teams cannot hope to be effective simply through adopting 'command and control' leadership tactics. They can, of course, set a strategic direction and negotiate guidelines and expectations with their team members, but at the end of the day effective performance in virtual teamwork relies heavily on trust and communication[20]. It is often assumed that if people work for the same company, share the same company values and work for a common goal, all this is enough to ensure that there will be trust among team members. But the reality is this: if you don't have the chance to build any kind of relationship with another person, it becomes very hard to trust him or her.

18 Crandell C., "What Does Trust Have To Do With Anything?", Forbes, 2012
19 Greenberg P.S., H. Greenberg R., Lederer Antonucci Y., "Creating and Sustaining Trust in Virtual Teams", Business Horizons (2007) 50, 325–333
20 Brake T., "Where in the World is my Team?", Jossey-Bass, 2008

CHAPTER 2 THE IMPLICATIONS OF CULTURE IN CROSS-CULTURAL VIRTUAL TEAMS

So how to establish that vital ingredient of trust in your virtual, and culturally-diverse team?

You will not be surprised to learn that the way trust is established and maintained also varies greatly in different cultures, so developing trust among your team members it is not necessarily a straightforward business. Some cultures are comfortable starting off by trusting everyone until proven differently, while in other cultures, trust is not necessarily freely given, but needs to be earned first.

In the virtual setting, where nonverbal cues may be absent, the challenge of establishing trust may be even more pronounced. As Meyer (2014)[21], mentioned: "Most of us send an e-mail, or pick up the telephone without giving culture much thought. However, putting a little effort into the choice can help tremendously when you need to build trust with your globally dispersed colleagues". In the same article, Meyer also proposes a distinction between two different types of trust:

- **"Cognitive trust"**, often built through business interactions, and based on the confidence you feel in another person 's accomplishments, skills, and reliability

- **"Affective trust"**, which arises from feelings of emotional closeness, empathy or friendship and is usually built up through personal interactions.

It's not difficult to see from this distinction that the two types of trust presented closely relate to whether a culture is more task-oriented or relationship-oriented. Cultures like China or Brazil, which are rather relationship-oriented, feel that they can trust a colleague or business partner if they have a history of relationship with that person. On the other side, task-oriented cultures such as USA or Germany gain trust by knowing that the person is reliable and consistent in their work. Trust can be also analysed through **Hofstede 's five cultural dimensions**[22] which individually have effects on performance and also effects on leadership[23].

---

[21] Meyer E., "The Culture Map: Breaking Through the Invisible Boundaries of Global Business", Public Affairs, 2014, p. 189
[22] Hofstede G., Hofstede G.H., Minkov M., "Cultures and Organisations: Software of the Mind", 3rd Edition, McGraw-Hill USA, 2010
[23] Duarte D. L., Tennant Snyder N., "Mastering Virtual Teams: Strategies Tools and Techniques that Succeed, Jossey-Bass, 2006 p 149-153

HOFSTEDE'S FIVE CULTURAL DIMENSIONS

Power Distance: how far less powerful group members expect/accept power is distributed unequally	**High-PD:** more coercive and referent power is used. Power Distance Index scored as 104 in Hofstede sample	**Low-PD:** more reward, legitimate, and expert power is used. Power Distance index scored as 11 in Hofstede sample
Individualism/ Collectivism	**Individualism:** ties between individuals are loose: everyone expected to look after themselves and their immediate family	**Collectivism:** integration from birth into strong, cohesive in-groups protecting members in exchange for unquestioning loyalty
Masculinity/ Femininity: distribution of roles between genders	**High-M:** men's values very assertive and competitive; maximally different from women's values	**High-F:** men's values modest and caring and similar to women's values
Uncertainty Avoidance	**High:** acceptance of familiar risks; fear of ambiguous situations and of unfamiliar risks	**Low:** comfortable with ambiguous situations and unfamiliar risks
Long term/ Short term Orientation	**Long-term:** values of thrift and perseverance	**Short-term:** values of respect for tradition, fulfilling social obligations saving 'face'

Fig. 9: Source: www.ecute.eu/theory/synthetic-cultures/

CHAPTER 2 THE IMPLICATIONS OF CULTURE IN CROSS-CULTURAL VIRTUAL TEAMS

Firstly, those from **'high power distance'** countries may be more willing to accept authority from leadership figures, and, within cultures which value a high level of power distance, trust in leaders may be closely related to their decision-making ability.
In contrast, the opposite may well be the case for those in **'low power distance'** countries, where decision-making may be devolved throughout an organisation. In cultures where power distance is high, organisations tend to be more hierarchical and decision-making responsibility is often held at the upper echelons of leadership. Organisational structure within cultures favouring low power distance tend to be much 'flatter', so that people at all levels are actively encouraged to contribute their ideas, make decisions, and challenge the choices of senior leaders when they feel so inclined.

Looking at Hofstede's **uncertainty avoidance**[24] dimension, people from cultures with a high preference for 'uncertainty avoidance' may desire a clearly structured team process for the entire duration of the project, while those from cultures with a low need to avoid uncertainty may see this as a sign of weakness or anxiety which might have a detrimental impact on the team and the trust established within it. Useful tools in managing cultural variations in need for uncertainty avoidance might include keeping in constant communication with those people who liked to be informed about tasks, deadlines, procedures and structures. In this way, people who need to know that structure is being adhered to (or to be updated when it is not) will feel their discomfort at any 'change in the plan' is being dealt with sensitively, and may therefore feel more able to relax with the changes a little more.

The extent to which a culture is **individualistic or collectivist** influences (for example) the extent to which the team leader gains trust by getting involved in individual team members' career progression, or not, and the assistance team members might receive towards their individual career goals. This is particularly apparent in individualistic cultures where the focus is on the individual rather than the collective. However, in collective cultures where there is a stronger emphasis on the importance of the community, group or team, and where achievement is valued as a collective rather than an individual experience, trust is likely to be generated where team leaders show appreciation to the combined collaborative efforts of the whole team or group, rather than to separate people within it.

Overall, it seems pretty obvious from the points above that trust is a key element for any kind of team to operative effectively, virtual or not, and some commentators such as Lencioni (2002)[25] mention that an **absence of trust is the most critical dysfunction that a team can have.** Without trust, productive work and growth are almost impossible. Team members spend time and energy protecting themselves or undermining each other, instead of focusing on the work and goals of the team. As Lencioni puts it, *"Trust requires team members to make themselves vulnerable to one another, and be confident that their respective vulnerabilities will not*

---

24 Hofstede G., Hofstede G.H., Minkov M., "Cultures and Organisations: Software of the Mind", 3rd Edition, McGraw-Hill USA, 2010
25 Lencioni P. M., "The Five Dysfunctions of a Team: A Leadership Fable" 2002

be used against them. (...) It is only when team members are truly comfortable being exposed to one another that they begin to act without concern for protecting themselves". Lencioni goes on to state that trust generally grows in a working atmosphere when mistakes are accepted and forgiven, and where individuals are not singled out for blame, but rather everyone in the team is encouraged to think about errors in a constructive way.

The role of the leader is clearly very critical in setting the pattern here, and despite cultural differences, there are some general behaviours that leaders can put into practice to influence the development of trust. As presented in Duarte and Tennant Snyder's book, Mastering Virtual Teams[26], **acting with integrity** ensures that values and actions are aligned, and that virtual team members share, believe in, and act upon these values. Other ideas that are generally useful in any culturally-diverse team setting include following up on promises made, and being an example for other team members. The point about keeping your promises is especially important in a virtual team, because your word is often all you can give in a virtual environment.

The feeling of being out of the information-sharing process may also affect trust, making it highly important to **communicate openly and create an environment of inclusion**, regardless of where team members are based. Small oversights can cause surprisingly big setbacks in virtual space – people may feel excluded by not being copied in on an email, say, or by not having their presence noted or openly acknowledged at a meeting.

Some ways for virtual leaders to avoid inadvertently excluding any team members include:

- Using "starter questions" at the beginning of a meeting, in order to enable all participants to have an opportunity to introduce themselves and also to comment on a particular topic.

- Maintaining transparency with and within the team about any relevant information you need to share with them.

- Sharing information immediately with the group, as the quicker and the more you share, the more people will feel like sharing themselves, and, just as important in virtual space, you will avoid any assumptions from others that you may have a hidden agenda.

- Openly and efficiently communicating the correct information to all team members in a fair, neutral and timely manner and via an appropriate channel. Email messages, for example, are notoriously prone to being misconstrued if they are over-used, or used inappropriately, even given cultural variance on relevant uses of email and other written communication channels. In virtual space as in face to face contact, written communication should be clear and impartially-worded, in order to prevent misunderstandings or breakdown of trust due to recipients "reading between the lines" or generally misinterpreting the tone of the message.

---

26 Duarte D. L., Tennant Snyder N., "Mastering Virtual Teams: Strategies Tools and Techniques that Succeed", Jossey-Bass, 3rd edition 2006, p. 139-143

CHAPTER 3 LEADING HIGH-PERFORMING VIRTUAL TEAMS

And last but not least, **ensuring the well-being of others** may bring trust in a team when team members feel confident that the organisation, and their leader, is going to do the right thing to help them in any situation. In this, showing interest in each team member, by taking care to ask how they are feeling within their job and role, and how they are doing in general within the team, are invaluable steps to establishing a comfortable and productive atmosphere in your virtual team.

3.1. THE ROLE OF THE LEADER

Leadership is important in any team, but virtual teams have many special aspects that makes it even more important. As Caulat clearly points out: *"the crucial differentiator between mediocre and high performing virtual teams is the development of virtual leaders who are able to develop and lead virtual teams. Effective management of virtual teams is necessary but not sufficient: there is a real need for virtual leadership"*[27].

There is still the tendency to believe that to be a successful virtual leader means being able to translate good leadership skills into a virtual setting. However, virtual 'dynamics' are much more complex than many leaders believe: new skills and characteristics are required to be successful here. There is no blueprint for success either for traditional teams or for virtual teams and there is also no great difference in the leadership style required for these. However, one key attribute of successful "virtual leaders" is to **be more of a facilitator than a supervisor.** What does this suggest? It means that one of the biggest tasks facing virtual leaders is to transform themselves from directors into facilitators, who are capable of coaching, managing, motivating and empowering their team members, as well as (when needed) giving them clear direction.

Combining the outcomes of our Doujak surveys from 2010 until 2014 with our practical experience in working with virtual team leaders and their teams, we identified **4 main competences that a virtual leader should possess**, as described in the graph.

---

27 G. Caulat, "Virtual Leadership", The Ashridge Journal, Autumn 2006.

- Comfort with the technology
- Ability to fix small technological problems
- Ability to choose the right technology for the team and situation

- Relationship building and good networking skills to stay connected, focusing also on virtual social interactions
- Cultural sensitivity and ability to work with different cultures
- Ability to foster intercultural understanding in the team
- Problem-solving and conflict resolution skills

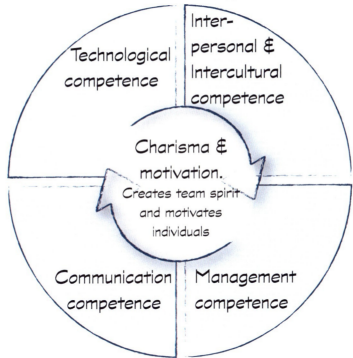

- Has an adaptable communication style according to the situation
- Quick to share information and react to questions.
- Transparent communication process.

- Has an adaptable communication style according to the situation
- Quick to share information and react to questions.
- Transparent communication process.

Fig.: 10: Competences and Skills for Successful Virtual Leaders. © Doujak Corporate Development

CHAPTER 3 LEADING HIGH-PERFORMING VIRTUAL TEAMS

The leader has many **responsibilities** when facilitating a virtual team. She has to establish the credibility of team members, help peers to get to know each other, provide a sense of unity, anticipate the needs of the team from a cultural and communication standpoint, make sure that everyone is equally involved and actively participating in the project, and overcome technology gaps across team members.

All of this may sound like quite a tall order, but we haven't finished yet! The virtual leader also has to spend more time talking with his people, and particularly giving team members recognition and understanding that their contribution is valuable, indeed critical for success.
As already mentioned, one of the biggest challenges for virtual teams is reduced personal contact with others, which could lead to misunderstandings and sometimes isolation of team members. An active team leader who invests time in personal contact with the people in the team and gives them positive feedback and a sense of belonging plays an important role in bridging the technological and geographical gap.

Finally, the leader needs a finely-tuned understanding of the different levels of communication within, and the complexity of, the virtual environment. This means that he will need to put even more thought into setting up and running virtual meetings than might be necessary for face to face ones, to make them as effective and productive as possible by paying attention to the tools/technologies used, the time-frame and time zones involved, who it is necessary to invite, having a realistic and relevant agenda, keeping it socially engaging – and so on.

In general many managers say that **meeting each other face to face** at least once can already make a big difference to team collaboration. Building and maintaining trust among team members, if they have had the opportunity to meet at least once, makes everything much easier as it fosters mutual understanding and social connection. If you have the chance to bring everyone together in the same place, face to face meetings could be useful for all kinds of occasions, including: 'kick off' meetings, milestone meetings, wrap-up or celebration meetings, performance reviews, conflict resolution – and so on. The choice is extensive!

Is it possible to lead people and build trust in a virtual team without any face to face contact?
We believe that it is. However, in the absence of face to face contact, good communication is key to building relationships and establishing trust. This may include a personal phone call to give feedback to each team member and making sure nobody gets cut out from the information sharing.

BUILDING TRUST AND COLLABORATION

HERE ARE SOME ADDITIONAL TIPS TO BUILD TRUST AND COLLABORATION IN A VIRTUAL TEAM

- **Establishing individual team members' roles and responsibilities upfront** is vital. In doing this, try to ensure you don't have duplication of work and also that tasks are not 'falling down between the cracks in the floorboards'. This is much more difficult to ensure when the team members aren't situated right outside your door.

- **Agree on targets, constraints, terminology, standard templates, standard formats, procedures and processes upfront.** Setting standard process and content delivery information from the start, and also milestones and specific outcomes or deliverables, is one crucial way to help people in your team feel fully confident that they know your expectations, and the role they have been assigned. Without this kind of structure, many team members working virtually may feel as though they are being repeatedly 'pumped' for information on an ad hoc basis.

- For many team members there may already be a feeling of isolation, particularly if they are less used to the virtual environment. In these circumstances, it's important for team members to build bonds quickly, and it may be helpful **to stretch your usual rules of communication, for example not to quibble over communication tools such as e-mail being used to make contact and build social relationships.** It's best that people use available communication tools (even those usually less preferred for social contact, like email) in the early stages of a virtual team's formation in order for trust to be encouraged rather than stifled.

- Try to have a **local manager or at least a local person responsible** for each local team to offer guidance, support and direction from a local perspective and remember to stick to the decisions made jointly with the group.

- Ensure team members are **comfortable with the chosen technology** and communication tools.

- The use of **project management information systems** will greatly increase the ability of remote team members to directly access the latest project status in "real time".

- This should be expanded to include a key document repository for all team members to access, as well as an associated **document sharing software or system** (ex. Dropbox, Sharepoint, etc) to ensure everyone is getting the same information.

CHAPTER 3 LEADING HIGH-PERFORMING VIRTUAL TEAMS

- **Define the core "time slots" in each day when shifts of personnel overlap,** and therefore synchronous communication can take place. While it's important to highlight the need for availability at these key times, it's also very helpful to be flexible, so that people can attend outside these times when needed. Even if there are no specific project requirements to discuss, just saying hello and exchanging niceties maintains the contact and involvement of remote team members and makes them feel equally valued and involved.

In the next graph we describe some **team dynamics that a virtual leader should encourage.** The leader has to support an environment where:

- People can **share** information, documents and personal information.
- People constantly **learn** from each other, about each other, and feel they are developing themselves in their job.
- The team is motivated by the **leader celebrating and acknowledging successes.**
- **Social relationships** within the team are actively fostered and supported.
- **People feel fully involved**, and want to be part of things.

DYNAMICS THE LEADER SHOULD ENCOURAGE

SHARING

- Meet frequently
- Make it interactive
- Work together in real time
- Make it visual
- Make coffee breaks
- Use the tools to share and make it visual, e.g. mind mapping, white boards, power point

LEARNING

- Be a learning team
- Have a pilot process to overcome technological barriers
- Adapt to local perspectives
- Get to know the people
- Encourage global training programs
- Have fun and ongoing learning

MOTIVATING

- Focus on celebrating & recognitions
- Celebrate working together
- Inject some humor
- Be fair and equitable
- Develop things together while you are online: create ownership

ENHANCING RELATIONSHIPS

- Appreciate value & contribution per individual
- Help team members to know each other
- Have a good & clear team charter
- Keep the same level of hierarchy
- Meet personal needs
- Do regular team and individual communications
- Never forget the human factor

Fig. 11: Dynamics in Leadership Facilitation. © Doujak Corporate Development.

CHAPTER 3 LEADING HIGH-PERFORMING VIRTUAL TEAMS

3.2. BUILDING THE VIRTUAL TEAM

Virtual teams can be set up to fulfil many different purposes, but the most frequent ones are either functional teams which are spread geographically e.g. a global sales team consisting of sales people from the markets and the headquarters, or project teams which are set up for a specific period of time for a specific goal.

Defining the team is the first step of virtual collaboration and a key to success. The company culture, the required characteristics and skills of the team's members, and the type of team e.g. functional or project team, or some other kind again, – all these are of course important aspects that should be clearly defined in order to frame the purpose of the team.

When defining a team, you could ask yourself the following questions:

- Is the team going to be useful for internal purposes (e.g. have better coordination between business units) or external purposes (e.g. to provide a service to a client)?
- Is it a project team or a functional team?
- Will it operate across departments, organisations, countries or in fact globally?
- Is it a short-term or long-term assignment?

If you can answer these questions successfully, and it looks as though establishing a virtual team is indeed the answer to your business's needs, there are three more questions to consider:

- Is the company able to support and integrate the virtual approach into its working culture?
- Is it possible to gather the "best fit" team members to achieve the defined goal?
- What kind of technological setting is required to support effective collaboration?

Having the appropriate team members within the team clearly makes confidence and team-building easier to achieve, and thanks to the possibilities thrown open by virtual collaboration, team leaders now have the ability to draw on the best personnel from anywhere in the world to match project requirements, without being constrained to drawn upon a local 'pool' of talent. In many cases, choosing experienced professionals with global knowledge and expertise will be a considerable bonus, enabling your company to take advantage of the knowledge generated in its different business locations. Instead of having experts in each country, the company can combine experts, using the experience of different countries integrated into a global experience.

GETTING STARTED

When people gather together for the first time, roles and responsibilities are often unclear, there is little trust, and motivation might be low. There may be team members who question the legitimacy of the project, and, as people don't know each other, possibly some questions about whether or not the skills or experience required among team members for collaboration on this new project are actually available.

When starting up a team the initial objectives are to:

- Provide orientation;
- Start the process of building trust;
- Gain commitment from team members.

CHAPTER 3 LEADING HIGH-PERFORMING VIRTUAL TEAMS

SAMPLE PROCESS FOR BUILDING A TEAM

Based on our experience with a range of virtual team development projects, we would like to show you a **process which takes into consideration the three different levels of impact, upon individuals, teams and organisations.** In each of the 5 different **stages of team development** shown below you will find recommendations for possible interventions at all three levels. Please note that although we have divided these phases of development as shown, the five stages can also happen simultaneously.

After the illustration of the sample process, we have included a short description of **a case study describing the building up a global virtual team for a culture change project.** What started as a small initiative lead to a worldwide community supporting the implementation of new culture-related projects as well as a "hands on" business topics.

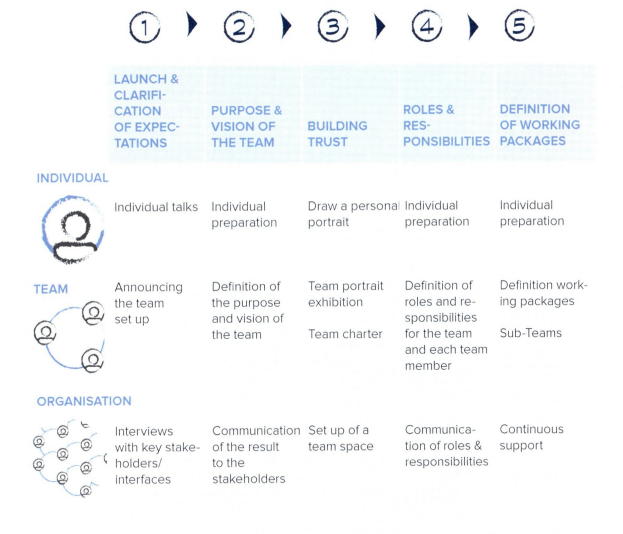

Fig. 12: Dynamics in Leadership Facilitation. © Doujak Corporate Development.

CHAPTER 3 LEADING HIGH-PERFORMING VIRTUAL TEAMS

TOOL: SAMPLE PROCESS FOR BUILDING A TEAM

PHASE 1: LAUNCH OF TEAM AND CLARIFICATION OF EXPECTATIONS

The main goal of this phase is to launch the team officially with a team "kick-off", and to start building up relationships with each team member. It is also the right time to clarify expectations all round: what the organisation seeks from the team, the team leader's expectations and also the varying hopes and needs of team members from their leader.

INDIVIDUAL LEVEL

WHAT TO DO:

INDIVIDUAL TALKS WITH EACH TEAM MEMBER

In order to get to know team members, the leader might consider the following questions:
- What do you as a leader expect from each team member?
- What does each team member need (from you as a leader and from team colleagues) to work efficiently in the team?
- What does each team member recognize as his/her main area of responsibility?
- Does this area of responsibility reflect the team member's range of skills and abilities?

WHICH TECHNOLOGY SHOULD BE USED FOR THIS?

Personal contact, through whatever channel, is crucial here because this is a relationship-building conversation. The team leader might therefore appropriately have the conversation via a phone call, a video conference, or, if possible of course, a face to face meeting.

TEAM LEVEL

WHAT TO DO:

ANNOUNCING THE SET-UP OF THE TEAM

This is the first time the team will get together, so the aim of this session should be to have a smooth start, and ensure that everyone has the opportunity to get to know each other, and feel comfortable joining the new team.

> **TOPICS THAT MIGHT BE IMPORTANT TO INCLUDE IN THE FIRST TEAM MEETING ARE:**
> - "Welcome to the team" - statement by the leader
> - Explanation of the main reason for the team's creation: "The reason why we are here is…"
> - Role of the team: "And that's why our main role and tasks will be…."
> - Expectations of the team by the various stakeholder groups: "When I got the job to put together the team, management told me that they expect the following…."
> - Team composition: Who is part of the team: "That's why I have selected you as team members…."
> - Team introduction: A short introduction of each team member
> - Your expectations and "offer" as a team leader:
>   "I am expecting from you …, and you can expect from me …"
> - Time for questions and discussion

WHICH TECHNOLOGY SHOULD BE USED FOR THIS?

The channel for this needs to enable document/file sharing, and a structure which allows time for questions and free-flowing discussion. Therefore a web meeting with slide share and/or video options might be a useful option here.

CHAPTER 3 LEADING HIGH-PERFORMING VIRTUAL TEAMS

TOOL: SAMPLE PROCESS FOR BUILDING A TEAM

ORGANISATIONAL LEVEL

WHAT TO DO:

TALKS WITH KEY STAKEHOLDERS/INTERFACES (DEPARTMENTS OR TEAMS YOU WILL COLLABORATE WITH IN THE FUTURE)

After the brief team 'set up' meeting where the main expectations have been discussed and clarified, it can sometimes be advisable – depending on the team composition and purpose – to have a further round of conversations where each team member talks to their main stakeholders/contacts. In matrix organisations, this could be their direct superior but it could also be other departments or teams they will collaborate with in the future. This is a highly valuable means to gather additional relevant information about stakeholder expectations, and additional relevant information for the team before the team gets down to business.

These stakeholder conversations will require

- a definition/understanding of who the main stakeholders are
- interviews to be carried out with the major stakeholders regarding their expectations of the team

WHICH TECHNOLOGY SHOULD BE USED FOR THIS?

This kind of conversation may be fairly relaxed and informal, and so could be achieved by a simple call or even a virtual coffee with the stakeholders.

PHASE 2: PURPOSE AND VISION OF THE TEAM

Now that the team members are on board and the initial 'kick off' meeting has taken place, it's time to define a joint purpose and vision for the team. The purpose defines the reason why the team exists. The vision defines what the team wants to achieve together. And here's the thing: in our experience, **teams which have a strong purpose and vision are more successful in reaching high performance.**

There may be several reasons for this. Teams with purpose and vision have a clearer idea of the direction they are heading in, and all their goals and tasks can be aligned according to this – so it is therefore easier to set priorities. If the main purpose and vision of the team is clearly defined and adopted by the team members, it enables them to be more flexible regarding how to achieve their goals/tasks. What follows from this is that teams with a strong, clear purpose and vision adjust to change more quickly than those which lack these elements.
So investing time in developing a joint purpose and vision for the team is not a phase to ignore or treat lightly – it needs an investment of time and energy to take this crucial step in laying the foundation for team cooperation and success.

CHAPTER 3 LEADING HIGH-PERFORMING VIRTUAL TEAMS

TOOL: SAMPLE PROCESS FOR BUILDING A TEAM

WHAT TO DO:

INDIVIDUAL PREPARATION

Evaluation of the main points of the interviews, taking into account the team member's specific expectations of the team, and development of appropriate conclusions from this.

Preparation task for each team member:

Based on the information I gathered from the interviews...

- I would see these 3 points as our main area of responsibility
- I would describe our team purpose as the following/ we exist for the following purpose...
- Our vision/what we want to achieve in the long run should be the following ..."

WHICH TECHNOLOGY SHOULD BE USED FOR THIS?

Individual/asynchronous work – if the team size is big, it might be helpful to ask team members to send their results upfront so that they can be consolidated for the team meeting.

WHAT TO DO:

TEAM MEETING TO DECIDE PURPOSE AND VISION

The team meeting this time has the aim to jointly discuss the information each team member has gathered, and also collaborate to define a purpose and vision for the team which all team members can commit and aspire to achieve.

AGENDA OF THE MEETING

Introduction and goals

Information gathering: each team member presents results and recommendations

Discussion:
- Looking at the results of the interviews, what are the similarities and differences?
- What becomes clear?
- What aspects are missing?
- Setting stakeholder needs aside for a moment, what is the team's personal picture of our purpose and vision?

Development of (a first draft for) the team purpose: Our team exists in order to ...

Development of (a first draft of) the vision: Our vision is to achieve the following....

Wrap up and next steps

CHAPTER 3 LEADING HIGH-PERFORMING VIRTUAL TEAMS

TOOL: SAMPLE PROCESS FOR BUILDING A TEAM

Depending on the size of the team, the complexity of the expectations, and the tasks involved, it might take several web meetings, with work in sub-groups in the interim, to develop the purpose and vision of the team as fully as needed. Our recommendation is that it is far better to invest time at this stage in order to achieve a sound purpose and vision to which everyone can commit, and to leave some additional time later for fine-tuning and further feedback and comments.

After defining the team's purpose and vision, the next stage is to identify the team's areas of responsibility and impact. In other words. This is what we offer/do…

Notably, some teams also find it useful to define what they don't do - which makes it easier for them to manage inappropriate stakeholder expectations at a later date.

WHICH TECHNOLOGY SHOULD BE USED FOR THIS?

A web meeting may work best here.

ORGANISATIONAL LEVEL

WHAT TO DO:

COMMUNICATION OF THE RESULTS TO STAKEHOLDERS

Once the team purpose and vision are defined it is time to 'position' the team externally. The positioning of the team for the rest of the organisation, especially key stakeholders or even to the external world on the one hand helps to strengthen the team identity but more important, it gives a clear statement to the external world regarding what to expect from the team, and what kind of services are offered. In return stakeholder team positioning talks can be used to negotiate what is needed from the stakeholders in order to successfully be able to achieve the goals. This process is often known as stakeholder management or expectation management.

WHICH TECHNOLOGY SHOULD BE USED FOR THIS?

Depending on the necessity for personal contact, possible ways of communication are:

- Create a page on the Intranet or any other internal page
- Write an official "Hello world e-mail"
- Organize a web meeting or videoconference which the main stakeholders are invited to join
- Organize stakeholder expectation management talks to give an update on the result of the interviews and the team positioning, and get into an expectation management dialogue.

CHAPTER 3 LEADING HIGH-PERFORMING VIRTUAL TEAMS

TOOL: SAMPLE PROCESS FOR BUILDING A TEAM

PHASE 3: BUILDING TRUST

As already mentioned, establishing trust is one of the main success factors for (virtual) teams, and all too often this crucial factor is paid too little attention, or entirely ignored when a virtual team is created. Having a single stage in the teambuilding process called "building trust" might be misleading, as in reality one trust building exercise alone is unlikely to achieve this. Generating trust among team members requires constant relationship-building between them, as well as a lot of time and sensitivity from the team leader in ensuring that important matters affecting relationships and social contact between team members are dealt with whenever the need arises.

In this phase of team development, we therefore suggest an exercise which can be planned and carried out as a first step in building trust in the virtual team.

INDIVIDUAL LEVEL

WHAT TO DO:

"TEAM PORTRAIT":

- Each team member gets an exercise to complete, which requires them to fill in a specific profile on the team space about themselves, following guiding questions that are shown on the team space. Their profile might include a photo, creative drawing or anything else which each individual thinks would be nice to share.
- As an outcome of this exercise everybody has a shared view of the job and responsibilities, working approach and leadership style of team colleagues – as well as some personal information.

Here are some questions you might consider using for this exercise:

1. This is me... You are invited to share some personal information, which your colleagues may not know yet. (Name, Picture, hobbies and private interests, dream job, what I am most proud of..., etc.)

2. My main professional achievements so far (Please write the most important 3-5 experiences you would like to share, which might be relevant for your new role - or even just interesting to share with your new colleagues!)

3. How would I describe my area of responsibility? What are the main tasks I fulfil? (You could name the main aspects of your job profile or any other information that you think is appropriate to share)

4. My working style... What do you need in order to work effectively – in general/from your team mates/from your team leader? For example - Are you more of a team 'brain-stormer', expressing your ideas freely as they come to you, or do you prefer to think things through first and then discuss it in the team when you have had time to reflect fully on your ideas? What are important values for you when working in a team? Which is your preferred way to communicate (e.g. aloud/vocally, or in writing?)

5. What kind of information do you require from others, in order to work efficiently?

6. My leadership style... (How do you lead others, and what do you expect from a leader?)

7. What's my definition of a "team"... (What do you think are the factors which make teams successful?)

8. The best 'high-performing' team I know/"dream team" (Please give an example, including a picture of that team – this could be your favourite football team, you and your husband, your former team etc. and explain in a maximum of 3 points what made it successful.)

WHICH TECHNOLOGY SHOULD BE USED FOR THIS?

For this purpose a team space or web page might be set up. Alternatively, each team member might have a 'profile template' to complete, which can then be uploaded so that everyone has access to the profiles of their peers.

CHAPTER 3 LEADING HIGH-PERFORMING VIRTUAL TEAMS

TOOL: SAMPLE PROCESS FOR BUILDING A TEAM

WHAT TO DO:

TEAM PORTRAIT EXHIBITION

As soon as the team portraits are online on the team space, team members are invited to take a look at their colleagues' portraits and get to know each other. Depending on the technology and communication style of the team members, this will ideally encourage people to comment on what they read, exchange common interests, and so on. By having all individual portraits combined on one page – hey presto, a 'team portrait' is created!

Apart from the team portrait 'exhibition' described here, a web meeting where each team member introduces the main points of their portrait, and others offer their comments on each portrait, could also be a great relationship-building activity.

WHICH TECHNOLOGY SHOULD BE USED FOR THIS?

A team space where people are able to post comments and feedback needed in order to achieve this – otherwise you could dedicate a web meeting to this activity, and invite further discussion.

WHAT TO DO:

DEVELOPMENT OF A TEAM CHARTER

The team portrait already contains important information on what people need in order to work effectively. After taking the time to define these needs, and share them with the team, the next step is to create a joint team charter which includes guidelines for collaboration and rules of communication, according to the following kinds of questions.

- Definition of team values: how do we want to work together?
- How do we agree to communicate? (Communication "rules")
- Which media to use, when and how (mails, chat, calls) and who to inform?
- Which meeting structure to apply: how often should we meet?

WHICH TECHNOLOGY SHOULD BE USED FOR THIS?

The team space can be used for a first 'brainstorm' on the main items to be included in the team charter. In order to get a fully collaborative commitment to the charter, a web meeting might be required where all team members can come together, carry out any final fine-tuning, and officially "sign off" the charter together.

CHAPTER 3 LEADING HIGH-PERFORMING VIRTUAL TEAMS

TOOL: SAMPLE PROCESS FOR BUILDING A TEAM

WHAT TO DO:

PROVIDE THE RELEVANT INFRASTRUCTURE

The task of the organisation at this stage is to provide the relevant infrastructure to make the team space possible.

WHICH TECHNOLOGY SHOULD BE USED FOR THIS?

Provide a team space or other file share system where people can share, interact, comment and jointly work on something online.

PHASE 4: ROLES AND RESPONSIBILITIES

Some high-performing teams are successful with roles and responsibilities that are only vaguely defined, because the level of trust and knowledge about each other's skills and way of working is so high that they intuitively respond to each other and work together. But this might be rather an exception. **So the overall rule remains: the clearer the roles and responsibilities of each team member, the more efficient the work can be.** In order to avoid misunderstandings and conflicts it is wise to define roles and responsibilities for the team as a whole and for each individual team member. At the same time it might also be useful to be open to changes and adaptations, depending on how tasks and timelines develop as the team gets into its stride.

WHAT TO DO:
JOB DESCRIPTION

Each team member writes a clear job description for him/herself and thinks of the following questions:

WHICH TECHNOLOGY SHOULD BE USED FOR THIS?

Individual, asynchronous work filling out a template.

My tasks ...

My roles and responsibilities ...

My main interfaces with team colleagues

My main interfaces with stakeholders

CHAPTER 3 LEADING HIGH-PERFORMING VIRTUAL TEAMS

TOOL: SAMPLE PROCESS FOR BUILDING A TEAM

WHAT TO DO:

ALIGNMENT OF ROLES AND RESPONSIBILITIES

The aim is to make the individual roles and responsibilities clear for each team member, and to ensure that the interfaces with other team colleagues and with stakeholders are clearly defined

It might also be useful to have a look at the overall profile of the team, and the roles and responsibilities of all team members.

WHICH TECHNOLOGY SHOULD BE USED FOR THIS?

Web-meeting or videoconference with slide-share facility.

ORGANISATIONAL LEVEL

WHAT TO DO:

ALIGNMENT OF ROLES AND RESPONSIBILITIES

Once the internal roles and responsibilities are clear, they should be conveyed to the rest of the organisation.

WHICH TECHNOLOGY SHOULD BE USED FOR THIS?

This could be done via

- an official communication on the intranet
- a personal mail to the stakeholders
- or individual phone calls

CHAPTER 3 LEADING HIGH-PERFORMING VIRTUAL TEAMS

TOOL: SAMPLE PROCESS FOR BUILDING A TEAM

PHASE 5: DEFINITION OF WORKING PACKAGES

This step focuses on the actual work. It starts with defining the main milestones and deliverables for the next few months and continues with concrete work 'packages' and assignment of tasks to team members. Here it might be advisable to split the team into sub-teams who work on separate issues in parallel.

WHAT TO DO:

GETTING READY FOR THE ACTUAL WORK

Now it's time to get ready for the actual work. Each team member could prepare for the team meeting by defining the main goals and tasks for the next months from his/her perspective.

WHICH TECHNOLOGY SHOULD BE USED FOR THIS?

This is a matter of individual, asynchronous preparation.

WHAT TO DO:

DEFINITION OF A 'ROADMAP' INCLUDING WORK PACKAGES VIA A WEB MEETING

Sample Agenda for this web meeting:

AGENDA OF THE WEB MEETING

1. Welcome and Intro

2. Goals: Our goals for the upcoming months?

3. Roadmap: Definition of the main milestones and deliverables for the next months

4. Work packages: Definition of work packages

5. Sub teams: Establishment of sub-teams who are either in the same location, or who work on the same subtopic. These sub-teams could have informal team leaders who would then coordinate the work.

WHICH TECHNOLOGY SHOULD BE USED FOR THIS?
Web-meeting or videoconference with slide-share facility.

ORGANISATIONAL LEVEL

In this phase continuous communication and support is required. On the one hand the task of the organisation is to support the team with the right environment to fulfil their tasks, on the other hand the team will have close interaction with other departments and teams due to interdependencies of the work or reporting guidelines. Therefore this actual working phase will require a lot of coordination and alignment and sometimes even conflict management with key stakeholders and the rest of the organisation. Once tasks are accomplished they need to be communicated and made visible.

CHAPTER 3 LEADING HIGH-PERFORMING VIRTUAL TEAMS

CASE STUDY: "BUILDING UP A GLOBAL VIRTUAL TEAM"[28]

THE STORY:

36 people from all over the world meet for the first time in a virtual meeting to start a global project. Its goal is to implement the target culture of a global automotive company worldwide.

They have never seen each other before. They will collaborate on joint initiatives virtually for the first time. The first personal meeting in the course of a workshop is planned after half a year.

Key players are involved from each region, who are invited to act as ambassadors by bringing in their local perspective and to act as 'multipliers' and 'communicators' for the culture project into their own organisation. The members of this change team receive tasks which they prepare together with their local colleagues, and subsequently present on the international level in webinars.

Instead of long journeys and 'presence days' in workshops, the communication is focused on 90-minute webinars. These webinars are created based on the "infotainment" principle, with a lot of drive, different formats and contributions which resemble an "early morning radio show" and create a very positive momentum.

The astonishing aspect of the first half year is that based on the continuous exchange between team members, a strong team culture is already being developed with qualitatively high performing results.

---

[28] A. Doujak, B. Heitger, Harte Schnitte Neues Wachstum: Wandel in Volatilen Zeiten. Die Macht der Zahlen und die Logik der Gefühle im Change Management, 2. Edition, 2014, p. 205-206

Trust and the relationships between the members as well as a successful working mode have emerged already.

The team spirit is further strengthened by an intensive two-day face-to-face workshop, in which the team members work on an implementation plan for the target culture and align this with the management team. The responsibility for implementation and the detailed design of the activities stay with the employees and their management in the countries. This local involvement turns out to be an essential factor in motivating individual countries to contribute.

Since then the team has continued its work on the different locations worldwide, supporting the implementation of new projects and the further development of related initiatives. The level of implementation positively astonishes many managers. The purely virtual network – the members have not met face to face since that one time – has been active for more than three years now and now forms an important part of the company-organisation. The community continues to grow, the members from the "early days" are partly being replaced by new people, in order to constantly bring fresh ideas in. And in terms of content there is a further development: after initially supporting culture-related topics, the network now also supports "hand on" business topics.

CHAPTER 3 LEADING HIGH-PERFORMING VIRTUAL TEAMS

3.3. GUIDELINES FOR LEADING VIRTUAL TEAMS

Once you have got the virtual team going, what can you do to keep it ticking over and performing as you want? Based on the extensive experience we have in virtual collaboration and a compilation of best practices noted over the years, we have prepared a list of practical tips on how to manage and lead a virtual team.

1. DEFINE CLEAR GOALS, ROLES AND AREAS OF RESPONSIBILITY

As we've mentioned already, and perhaps it bears repetition here, the definition of the team's purpose and the goals of its individuals together create the foundation of any team, whether face to face or virtual. And on top of that, the team needs to know what its job is, and who will make that happen – so clearly defining roles and areas of responsibility is crucial from the start – namely, who is in charge of what.

- Have each participant define **"My contribution to our success"** and then ask them to share it with the rest of the team

- Review the **individual goals** on a regular basis to make sure people are still on the right track

2. CLEARLY DEFINE THE WORKFLOW AND SET UP A PROFESSIONAL PROJECT MANAGEMENT APPROACH

Here are some key questions for any virtual team regarding defining, and managing the flow of work to be undertaken according to project resources, desired outcomes and timelines.

- Who is working on what?
- When should any of these responsibilities be handed over, and to whom?
- What is the allotted timescale for the project?
- Are the expectations of the team members appropriate and realistic?

In terms of project management, the team should **regularly share updates on what they are currently working on,** where they have got to with any particular tasks, and what their workload looks like. For example, **having weekly updates** gives the team leader the opportunity to step in if one team member is overloaded with work, and shift this workload to another team member. Similarly, if a team member's motivation has clearly dropped, it is important to immediately call him or her to find out the reason and see what can be done to assist the person to get some energy and enthusiasm back.

These updates can be highly motivational and energising for all team members. At the same time, they also enable the team to learn together, and to share their achievements and successes, quite apart from the obvious function of keeping a continuous flow of communication and information between people, and highlighting any questions that need a response. Therefore it can quickly become an interactive and dynamic means of group or team communication.

Another useful project management tool is the **"virtual team space"**, which is essentially an "online storage room" of IT-strengthened links where people, being geographically dispersed, can communicate and interact with each other and where various documents can be stored, modified, and searched. Having a clear workflow and project management set up will make the team more efficient and also better interconnected. This could be a special team area on Sharepoint or an additional project management tool such as Dropbox, Box or Basecamp or any other corporate IT solution that is provided by the organisation.

CHAPTER 3 LEADING HIGH-PERFORMING VIRTUAL TEAMS

💡 **Establish sub team**s who are either in the same location or work on the same 'sub-topic'. These sub teams could have informal team leaders who would then coordinate the work

💡 **Weekly updates:** Agree that every team member should communicate an update at the end of the week. These updates may include items such as:

- Brief description of what they are working on
- Outlook for the next week regarding workload and required outputs
- Highlights of the week
- Workload: 1-10 (1=very low, 10= very high).
- Mood and motivation (1=very low, 10= very high).
- Other comments/something personal

💡 **Status updates:** invite people to share status updates to see what other team members are currently working on any point during the project. These updates may be used also to keep track of the work rate of individuals, or even to know where this person is travelling to, or when they have working hours (ex. "in Singapore from 1-5th May, in Paris from 6-8th May", or "Mon. 9–16, Tue. 9–17, Wed. 9–12"). Use a Chat function like Skype, internal Facebook, and specific area on the team space or on any other media which enables sharing of status updates.

💡 **Team space:** set up a team space where team members can store and share documents. The team space should also be used to share updates on completed tasks, what people are currently working on and have a Chat function for quick questions. In order to make it more "personal", the space should also be used to share in order to make it more "personal", the space should also be used to share pictures and private information, and should serve as a reminder that you are part of a team and can meet the other team members quickly and easily in that virtual space.

3. SET UP CLEAR RULES FOR INTERACTION AND COMMUNICATION (TEAM CHARTER)

Setting up clear rules at the beginning will make it easier for the team to interact and communicate. We suggest developing a **"team charter"** together with the team, where you can agree on general **team values and rules for interaction**. Furthermore, having the rules noted on paper is not, on its own, enough. Make sure that these rules are actually lived in practice, by leading by example as a team leader, and by constantly reviewing them together with your team.

- When conference calls are organised, be aware of **time zones** and rotate timings if necessary so that not always the same people need to get up very early in the morning

- **Plan regular update meetings** and planning sessions and also plan 'critical' update meetings before a particular project milestone or in a crucial phase of change

- Actively and consciously **discuss collaboration topics** within the team e.g.
  How do we want to 'live' our teamwork?
  Is our code of conduct still valid?

4. ENABLE AN "OPEN DOOR" POLICY, USING THE RIGHT "COMMUNICATION MIX"

After defining team and individual expectations, and discussing what team members need in order to feel comfortable, there should also be clarification about how and when the team leader and team members can be reached (time zones, communication media, etc.). It's important in this regard to take into consideration the cultural differences and individual preferences of those in your team with regards to choosing the communication medium.

CHAPTER 3 LEADING HIGH-PERFORMING VIRTUAL TEAMS

The adoption of an **"open door policy"** enables your team members to be available via different media (i.e. phone, chat, team space, Skype, e-mails, and so on). This tackles the potential problem of individual isolation as well as the challenge that team members are not able to have informal office chats with colleagues by the coffee machine, as they could when working in the same physical space.

Certain issues must also be addressed at this point, such as, for example, each individual's preference regarding the channel or medium of interaction. This communication media preference may vary considerably from one person to the next, depending on personality, and also on cultural background. By offering a broad range of communication channels with which team members can reach you, you manage to stay in contact with each of them without having them step out of their comfort zone by experiencing a new type of communication software. As a result of this increased comfort, conversations may very often be more open and productive, with firmer conclusions and deeper understandings of the issues being discussed.

- Consider cultural and individual **communication preferences:** one person may feel more comfortable in writing e-mails, another team member may prefer talking personally on the phone while yet another may prefer chatting and instant messaging for quick and precise exchanges.

- **Use the right media for the right purpose:** define which communication tools are used when and how (for example, when writing e-mails consider who should be copied in, and how to indicate that something is urgent).

- Clarify which **virtual tools** to use for which **purpose**, when to use a webcam, and so on.

5. ESTABLISH OPENNESS BY ACTIVELY PROMOTING SOCIABLE COMMUNICATION

Informal and personal communication is a significant part of the virtual interaction, and should not be neglected. Why? When you consider the kind of sociable, informal conversation which typically takes place in face to face working at the coffee machine or when "bumping into" colleagues in the corridor, you realise that these kinds of friendly encounters are very important, and provide opportunities for building relationships and developing trust which very often just do not happen in a virtual environment, even though they make a significant difference to team collaboration.

In order to overcome this potential challenge, virtual leaders should try to actively plan regular informal networking activities within the team at least once a month. The "Tips" box below gives some simple and practical suggestions for effective ways to do this.

- During meetings make a point of asking **'relationship-oriented' questions** to initiate small talk, e.g. "How is the weather in Dubai?", "Did you have a nice weekend?", "How was your vacation – where did you go?" and so on.

- Actively plan regular **informal networking activities** within the team at least once a month. You might ask to have a "virtual coffee" with a colleague either via a virtual meeting, on the phone or in a video conference.

- Use **"Chat rooms"** to encourage informal collaboration where informal queries can be asked and answered

CHAPTER 3 LEADING HIGH-PERFORMING VIRTUAL TEAMS

6. TREAT ALL TEAM MEMBERS EQUALLY.

Within a virtual team there is a particular risk that some people may feel that they are not being treated equally, if they notice that they are not being updated by the leader at the same time as everyone else. And it clearly is a significant challenge in the virtual environment to hold back from first informing the team members who are based together on site, and then relying on informing geographically-dispersed others via a quick conference call or email.

With a face to face team you would just organize a quick meeting where everybody could participate equally, and nobody would have the feeling of being excluded. Perceived inequalities such as these, if left undiscussed and unmanaged, can quite rapidly lead to conflicts. In order to avoid imbalances, it is crucial to inform all team members at the same time.

- Send **minutes of meetings** to all those who are involved regardless of their participation in the meeting

- Equal communication to ALL team members regardless of their proximity or distance to the team leader. This means - do NOT inform or discuss information with the team members on site first but **try to inform all team members at the same time.** You can agree on a specific tool to use when sharing important or urgent information (e.g. sending out an e-mail with "urgent" in the subject line, meaning that everybody needs to react quickly to it).

7. KEEP A STRONG FOCUS ON SOCIAL DYNAMICS TO PREVENT ISOLATION OF TEAM MEMBERS.

Being located all over the world with little face-to face-contact can make people feel lonely and isolated. Remember to encourage and give opportunities for the team members to get to know you and each other. This will not only improve the feeling of being part of a real team, but it will also help to prevent any feelings of isolation and the possibility of conflict.

Here are some further ideas about ways to do this.

- **Create a team site/space** which exists alongside day to day work and business communication-related tools. The purpose of the team web-space is to provide a common identity for team members who don't frequently interact face to face. This page could include the team portrait.

- Create **"cyber cafes"** on the company intranet where people can stay in touch virtually and talk informally. This might reduce feelings of isolation and even foster creativity and learning across distance.

- Encourage virtual team members to use **visual reminders** of the team which could be a team picture or a team symbol. This really does make a significant difference in helping those people feel part of the team even when not physically connected.

- Use **webcams** also transmitting the **sound** of the office where the team member is located. This will enable the people who are not located on site to have an impression of what is going on through "hearing" the background noise of people at work, and thus feel more connected and involved in consequence

- Promote a **"hotel-style" room booking system** where people who usually work from home have the opportunity to reserve a working space or meeting room in the company, either for just a few hours or for a full day at a time.

CHAPTER 3 LEADING HIGH-PERFORMING VIRTUAL TEAMS

8. TAKE INTO CONSIDERATION INTERCULTURAL ASPECTS

If a team is virtual, it is often also multinational. It's particularly important for virtual team leaders to take into account the different cultural backgrounds of team members, and effects that this may have on decision-making, feedback and communication. Most of all treat each member with the same amount of dignity and respect. A further cultural variance may be the extent to which 'losing face' makes a difference in communication, for example whether it is acceptable to discuss personal performance or discipline a team member in person or in public. Managing cultural differences may also take the form of meeting rituals, which may differ considerably from nationality to nationality, in the same way as standards of punctuality, how information is exchanged and the variety of ways in which agreements are reached and consolidated.

- **Sharing of office cultures: It can be a great idea to** have each team member share what is "typical" in their office, for example – the usual working hours, lunch times, office structure, etc... This will increase mutual understanding within the team.

- **Present your own culture:** once per quarter have one team member sharing a virtual presentation about his/her own culture, including business aspects, such as communication style (direct vs indirect), giving feedback and power distance (hierarchical vs flat organisation) and so on.

9. ACTIVELY CELEBRATE SUCCESSES.

The celebration of achievements is often neglected and forgotten, particularly within virtual teams, where it is generally trickier to organise celebratory events! This makes it all the more important a requirement of the virtual team leader.

There are plenty of difficulties in expressing gratitude in words from a distance, but you are likely to find that a 'virtual celebratory cake' is one way - or even sending a real one! And remember, if you are a successful team, it is probable that the virtual team will be asked to repeat the process again for further projects, so don't see the end of the collaboration as closure but perhaps a pause until the next project.

Virtual applause: use a video/audio clip of people applauding (this can be found easily on Youtube) and play it during the team meeting.

Have a virtual party through **"online awards for special achievements"**.

"Thank you awards" for special support within the team which could possibly be linked to real prizes.

Make it "real": Be inventive when celebrating! Don't just send a "thank you" email, instead try to exchange a tangible present such as a bottle of wine or a cake, in order to replicate that celebratory drink which is missing from the end of the virtual team project. This kind of gesture encourages trust and a sense of belonging to the group, as well as a real share in group achievements.

CHAPTER 3 LEADING HIGH-PERFORMING VIRTUAL TEAMS

10. DEALING WITH HIDDEN CONFLICT

Conflict should not necessarily always be seen as a problem for team performance, as disagreements, even heated ones, may indicate that team members feel comfortable enough with each other to express their dissatisfaction openly and honestly.

Dealing with conflict varies from culture to culture. Whether it is settled in public or whether it is talked about in private meetings, the way conflict is viewed, and managed, is influenced by cultural distinctions, and what is known about the different personalities and behaviours involved for the duration of the conflict. In order to manage conflict effectively, there should be a process established. The main aim for conflict resolution should be for the process to be quick, inclusive and for it to not damage working conditions and results for the rest of the team and project. Above all, no matter how significant the differences or disagreements between team members may be, conflict cannot be ignored, but must be solved and discussed. Depending on the cultural aspects of the team, openness about resolving conflict will serve as a sign to other team members to be honest and upfront, but at the same time constructive in what they propose.

Another word on this. It's important to remember that in some contexts, conflict can actually be useful, such as when it takes the form of significant differences of opinion. When this occurs, the differences can be channelled positively in order to create a broad spectrum of innovative possibilities and thereby optimise the outcomes of teamwork.
There is nothing more lacking in creativity (and often unproductive) than a team whose members all agree with each other all the time, and think along pretty much the same lines. In contrast, a productive team environment is one where diverse views from all angles are welcomed, and a working atmosphere which values every team member's opinions is created.

Finally it should be said that the greater sense of confidence which some team members may get when working virtually may sometimes result in greater disagreements – mostly, rather ironically, because they feel comfortable discussing differences and airing their divergent views in the group!

💡 Be aware of possible hidden conflicts. **Actively address "hot topics"** and create an atmosphere where people can openly talk about their problems.

💡 Actively agree with the team on **"how we want to deal with conflicts"** (this can be part of the team charter).

💡 **Resolve conflicts quickly:** the process should be clearly defined with stages such as problem definition, possible solutions, exploration of consequences, settlement of any conflict which may have arisen during the process, and lastly a decision by mutual consent.

CHAPTER 3 LEADING HIGH-PERFORMING VIRTUAL TEAMS

3.4. ASSESSING YOUR VIRTUAL TEAM PERFORMANCE

After having read all the tips and guidelines, you might be still left with one big question in front of you. And that is: **"So – where does my team stand in terms of team performance?"** Of all the topics we discuss here, this is of course one of the most important. It's a question which we believe needs to be considered on a regular basis, by taking a few steps back from your daily routine, and checking where the team stands. This applies just as much to new teams as to teams that have been working together for quite some time.

So, what measures might you use, and how to apply them?

The Doujak Virtual Team Performance Model © is one which evaluates and assesses virtual team performance and it is based on eight core areas, those that we consider most influence high performance in virtual teams and virtual collaboration in general.

For each of the eight core areas we have developed a set of questions to analyze different aspects of teamwork, and determine a focus to further develop collaboration and reach high performance in a virtual team.

You can either use the checklist below as first self-assessment or assessment with your team or follow the suggested process below which also contains an online survey and a detailed analysis of your team.

Fig. 13: Doujak Virtual Team Performance Model © Doujak Corporate Development.

CHAPTER 3 LEADING HIGH-PERFORMING VIRTUAL TEAMS

VIRTUAL TEAM PERFORMANCE SELF-ASSESSMENT

Each core area is described and equipped with a self-assessment key which you could ask yourself or ask your team members to fill out. Having completed the questions, you could discuss with your team members where they see the biggest strengths of the team and where they would see areas of improvement. This could then be followed by a joint development of ideas on how to improve the respective competencies and consequently reach higher performance within the virtual team.

1. GLOBAL LEADERSHIP

describes how the leader supports the team and each team member in their role. The leader should set clear expectations, be accessible and proactive in sharing information, and clarify preferred channels of communication. She should also seek opportunities for formal and informal conversations, and make sure team members do not feel isolated. All of this in turn suggests that the leader will need some knowledge and understanding in working with people from different cultures, and also the ability to adapt her style according to each team member´s culture and needs. The potential and professional development of each individual team member should also be a focus, and she should build on the differences of the team members. Last but not least, the leader should create a team spirit and give a sense of security when dealing with unknown situations and challenging, conflictual issues.

This self-assessment part includes a lot of feedback questions for the team leader which are also interrelated with the other core competency areas of our Doujak Virtual Team Performance model. Therefore this self-assessment question is a bit more extensive than the other sections.

SELF-ASSESSMENT QUESTIONS FOR GLOBAL LEADERSHIP

	1	2	3	4	5	6	7	8	9	10
My leader fully supports me in my work	●	●	●	●	●	●	●	●	●	●
It is clear for me what my leader expects from me	●	●	●	●	●	●	●	●	●	●
My leader is reachable through different media (telephone, e-mail, Skype, etc.)	●	●	●	●	●	●	●	●	●	●
My leader actively seeks opportunities for informal and formal exchange	●	●	●	●	●	●	●	●	●	●
Within the team the leader takes care that no team member experiences isolation	●	●	●	●	●	●	●	●	●	●
I have the feeling that my leader can deal well with solving conflicts	●	●	●	●	●	●	●	●	●	●
My leader chooses the appropriate communication channels for our collaboration	●	●	●	●	●	●	●	●	●	●
My leader can switch communication style according to the team member's culture background and communication needs	●	●	●	●	●	●	●	●	●	●
My leader takes time to understand my cultural background and local situation	●	●	●	●	●	●	●	●	●	●
My leader is able to work with people from different cultural backgrounds	●	●	●	●	●	●	●	●	●	●

CHAPTER 3 LEADING HIGH-PERFORMING VIRTUAL TEAMS

SELF-ASSESSMENT QUESTIONS FOR GLOBAL LEADERSHIP

	1	2	3	4	5	6	7	8	9	10
My leader is always available when I need him/her	○	○	○	○	○	○	○	○	○	○
My leader answers my questions within an appropriate timespan	○	○	○	○	○	○	○	○	○	○
My leader has developed and promoted a sharing structure for the team	○	○	○	○	○	○	○	○	○	○
My leader promotes development of our team	○	○	○	○	○	○	○	○	○	○
I have the feeling that my individual potential is being fully used	○	○	○	○	○	○	○	○	○	○
My leader makes sure that, despite the distance, the team builds up a relationship and grows together	○	○	○	○	○	○	○	○	○	○
My leader sees the differences in team members as an advantage	○	○	○	○	○	○	○	○	○	○
My leader adapts his/her leadership style according to individual needs	○	○	○	○	○	○	○	○	○	○
My team leader stands behind us and defends us towards others	○	○	○	○	○	○	○	○	○	○

2. PURPOSE AND VISION

describes how clear both the team's purpose is, and the role of each team member in accomplishing that purpose and working towards the overall vision for the team. The purpose of the team describes the reason why the team exists, whereas the vision refers to what the team aims to achieve.

As already mentioned in the sample process for building a team section, having a clear purpose and vision are key elements of high performing teams. Purpose and vision set a clear direction and enable a smooth alignment of goals and tasks and priority setting. If the main purpose and vision of the team is clearly defined and adopted by the team members, it thus enables them to be more flexible regarding how to achieve their goals/tasks. It follows from this that teams with a strong, clear purpose and vision adjust to change more quickly than those which lack these elements.

CHAPTER 3 LEADING HIGH-PERFORMING VIRTUAL TEAMS

SELF-ASSESSMENT QUESTIONS FOR PURPOSE AND VISION

3. TRUST

refers to the level of trust that exists among team members. The team should openly share information and feel that they can always rely on team colleagues. A trusting environment should be cultivated where failure is accepted and acknowledged and weaknesses permitted, without individual blame or scapegoating. Feeling involved and included in the conversations and information-sharing within the team is also an important part of trust. Additionally, supporting each other, celebrating successes and seeking to understand fellow team members more deeply are also important aspects that help to build and maintain trust.

SELF-ASSESSMENT QUESTIONS FOR TRUST

CHAPTER 3 LEADING HIGH-PERFORMING VIRTUAL TEAMS

4. KNOWLEDGE AND SKILLS LEVERAGE

refer to the extent to which the team practises knowledge-sharing and takes advantage of the numerous and different skills shown by all team members. It is not only about using the full potential of the team, it is also about assigning tasks according to people´s strengths and also knowing team member's unique talents and skills. Team members have therefore been chosen because of their perfect 'fit', through possessing the relevant knowledge and skills that are right and necessary for this particular team or have the opportunity to develop additionally required skills if necessary.

If this 'fit' of talent to task is appropriate, joint learning and development of both individuals and the team are promoted. Part of the skill leverage also includes meeting deadlines and balancing the work load. Thanks to good planning, the team also takes advantage of 24-hour working days due to time differences.

SELF-ASSESSMENT QUESTIONS FOR KNOWLEDGE AND SKILLS

	1	2	3	4	5	6	7	8	9	10
I have the feeling that my full potential is used in the team	👎	●	●	●	●	●	●	●	●	●	👍
I have an overview about special skills/knowledge other team members have	👎	●	●	●	●	●	●	●	●	●	👍
Team members have been chosen because of their perfect knowledge/skills fit for this team	👎	●	●	●	●	●	●	●	●	●	👍
We have regular sharing of knowledge within the team	👎	●	●	●	●	●	●	●	●	●	👍
We jointly support each other on further personal development	👎	●	●	●	●	●	●	●	●	●	👍
We spend time on developing as a team	👎	●	●	●	●	●	●	●	●	●	👍
We take advantage of 24 hour working days due to time differences	👎	●	●	●	●	●	●	●	●	●	👍
We never miss a deadline	👎	●	●	●	●	●	●	●	●	●	👍
We are punctual in following our plans/to do´s	👎	●	●	●	●	●	●	●	●	●	👍

CHAPTER 3 LEADING HIGH-PERFORMING VIRTUAL TEAMS

5. CULTURAL AWARENESS

describes the ability of the team to benefit from an international and intercultural exchange, and the extent and skills with which team members respect, and show their respect for, other cultural backgrounds. One aspect of this cultural awareness shows in an ongoing interest in learning about cultural differences and distinctions, and applying that knowledge when necessary – so that culturally aware team members might ask for clarification where there is a misunderstanding or conflict within the team, instead of merely assuming that it has arisen due to different individual approaches or personalities. People in the team also appreciate being part of an international working group, with people from all over the world; they actively take advantage of the diversity in the team.

SELF-ASSESSMENT QUESTIONS FOR CULTURAL AWARENESS

CHAPTER 3 LEADING HIGH-PERFORMING VIRTUAL TEAMS

6. COMMUNICATION AND TECHNOLOGICAL SKILLS

refers to the communications culture and structure in place to support the team. Meetings are efficient and effective, time is spent on social communication and interaction, and technology is an "enabler" rather than a challenge. There is also clarity and understanding about which tool to use for which kind of communication, and meetings are managed smoothly and realistically, without overload on individual and team time.
There is a transparent and effective decision-making process, which does not exclude any team members.

SELF-ASSESSMENT QUESTIONS FOR COMMUNICATION AND TECHNOLOGICAL SKILLS

CHAPTER 3 LEADING HIGH-PERFORMING VIRTUAL TEAMS

7. ROLES AND TEAM STRUCTURE

clearly describes individual and team roles in achieving the team's goals and vision. The clarity of individual roles and responsibilities, as well as the overall team structure, allows people to collaborate more effectively, knowing who is currently working on what. Resources are allocated properly and team members enjoy more independence because of the virtual set-up, yet they are well connected with their colleagues and stakeholders and do not feel isolated. The flexibility that the virtual team setting allows becomes an asset rather than a challenge, because there is a clear structure to follow.

SELF-ASSESSMENT QUESTIONS FOR ROLES AND TEAM STRUCTURE

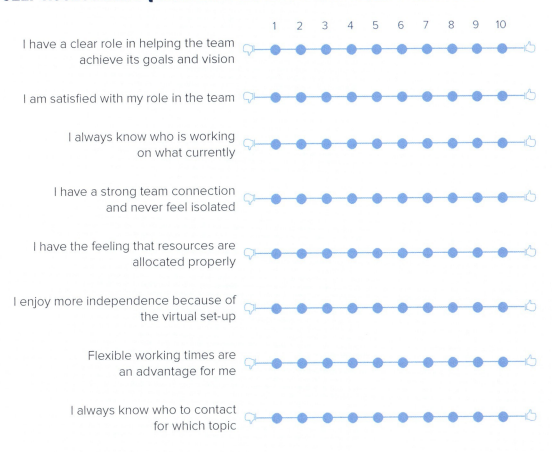

CHAPTER 3 LEADING HIGH-PERFORMING VIRTUAL TEAMS

8. ORGANISATIONAL CULTURE

describes the extent to which the organisation supports and encourages virtual working and provides teams with the necessary technical infrastructure and resources to achieve their goals. A truly global organisational culture embraces virtual working as part of every-day life and also supports culture diversity. Team members develop a strong feeling of "belonging" and feel supported in their tasks.

Please note that the areas 1–7 are all areas that the team leader and the team can influence directly. When it comes to organisational culture, the circle of influence is limited. Nevertheless we consider it an important part of the assessment, as it shows what the cultural environment is like in which virtual working will take place, and highlights possible organisational limitations which need to be considered.

SELF-ASSESSMENT QUESTIONS FOR ORGANISATIONAL CULTURE

CHAPTER 3 LEADING HIGH-PERFORMING VIRTUAL TEAMS

VIRTUAL TEAM PERFORMANCE ONLINE-ASSESSMENT

Now as you already know the different virtual team high performance areas, you might get caught by the thought that it would be much more useful to make an online assessment where each team member can fill in their opinion online and you automatically get the analysed result on where you stand and what you should be working on. Having had the same thought, we have developed an online assessment.

Here's how it works. Each team member (including the leader) completes an anonymous survey that covers the eight virtual team high performance areas. The results will be analysed by a consultant who then writes a team report for the leader highlighting the strengths and areas of development within the team, including recommendations on what to do next.

The next steps following the consultant's report very much depends on the team situation and areas of development: we usually advise team leaders to start with a one-to-one coaching session, and an explanation of the team report that includes some concrete tips for the leader. Bringing the team up to the next level of performance then requires energy to implement the required changes.

One way of doing this is to start with a one day team-building workshop (either face to face or virtual) where the results will be analysed and ideas for possible development can be developed by all team members.

While the assessment tool can be very useful for increasing cooperation and performance in a virtual team, it should be noted that in cases of particularly tough challenges (for example, enduring conflict or unresolved stress among particular team members), it is advisable to conduct one-to-one phone interviews with each team member to get a more in-depth view of the situation and make sure that the 'right' problem is being tackled.

The assessment can be repeated after a few months to see where there has been progress and which areas still have potential for improvement. This enables an ongoing development and learning process in reaching and containing high performance of a virtual team.

If you are interested in more information about the online virtual team performance assessment tool, please check the Doujak website or contact the authors directly.

CHAPTER 4 VIRTUAL MEETING FACILITATION

> *Virtual meetings are one of the most common ways for team members to meet, discuss, create, evaluate and make decisions.*
> *In order to make them efficient and effective, there are several aspects that need to be considered.*

CHAPTER 4 VIRTUAL MEETING FACILITATION

In any discussion about virtual collaboration, it is essential to mention virtual meeting facilitation, and that is the topic for this section of our book.

One of the key elements of virtual facilitation is, of course, the technology which makes it possible to communicate with colleagues across distance. And this is one of the most anxiety-causing elements of working virtually in the first place. As we may all know through hard experience, if the technology doesn't work well for us, then the communication cannot happen and we are left at best with some embarrassment in front of our colleagues during a live meeting or training situation. At worst, we are faced with the disaster of an important corporate message being miscommunicated, or even not communicated at all.

So mastering the **technology plays a highly important role in the virtual facilitation game**, starting from choosing the right tool or platform for your purpose, through knowing how to use it appropriately and – last but very definitely not least - also knowing how to deal with any technical problems that may arise. But mastering the technology on its own does not necessarily make a successful virtual facilitator. Just as the **virtual leader** needs a different set of skills in addition to those required by her face to face counterpart, so does the **virtual facilitator.** In order to make virtual meetings of any kind effective and also meaningful – whether they involve training, individual or team coaching, or business communication, we have collected some best practices which will be introduced to you in the course of this chapter.

4.1. MASTERING THE TECHNOLOGY

Let's start with the obvious: technology plays a very important role in virtual collaboration. Mastering it requires some knowledge and skills, certainly, and a good place to start is knowing which tools or internet platforms to use for your communication purpose.

On the right, we have listed a range of virtual collaboration tools, clustered here according to the 'type' of tool, and also to the most appropriate uses for each. As you can see from this list, it's possible to distinguish between collaborative, communication, organisation and community tools.

1. COLLABORATIVE TOOLS

— are the ones that support virtual collaboration most effectively in an interactive manner (Examples: WebEx, Adobe Connect, Smart Bridgit, virtual whiteboards, GoToMeeting, GoToWebinar, Mindjet, Skype for Business, videoconferencing).

2. COMMUNICATION TOOLS

— are very important tools when working virtually, but their function is more related to the coordination of activities or communication of important topics and not necessary to facilitating an interactive conversation across distance (Examples: MS Outlook, Skype, emails, phone calls, telephone conferences).

3. ORGANISATION TOOLS

— are important for the management of the team's time and tasks and to facilitate the information flow (Examples: MS Project, IBM Notes, Dropbox, MS SharePoint, functional databases).

4. COMMUNITY TOOLS

— are especially important for virtual teams, although, traditionally they are not seen as business tools. Their goal is to facilitate the social interaction of team members. Some examples of external tools are mentioned below, but most commonly special corporate tools are used for this purpose (YouTube, Twitter, Facebook, IBM connections, forums, blogs, Wikis).

CHAPTER 4 VIRTUAL MEETING FACILITATION

CHOOSING THE RIGHT VIRTUAL MEETING TOOL

The main difference between a face to face meeting and a virtual meeting is the additional complexity which arises from using technology. This may mean that the facilitator needs to be trained in the use of specific technology tools and/or software packages, such as video conference technology, virtual presentation features, conference call software, or something else. And of course the level of training required will vary according to the facilitator's familiarity with the tool in the first place, as well as the relevance of each of the services to the level of interaction required in the meeting.

The **level of interaction** varies across the different tools available. Some tools allow higher interaction, while others offer a lower interaction level. Why is this relevant? Depending on the **purpose of the meeting** and the goal of each agenda item, you may need a lower or higher level of interaction among participants.

Possible meeting purposes can of course be as broad-ranging as information-sharing, discussion, brainstorming, co-creation and development of ideas, decision-making, and so forth – all requiring varying levels of active participation from those attending. Taking a few examples to illustrate this, an information-sharing session will not necessarily require a high level of interaction, so a web-meeting solution where participants can interact only through voice and chat box will be enough. However, for meetings where the purpose is to engage in brainstorming activities, make decisions and work collaboratively, a higher level of interaction and therefore more technology features might be required.

Another factor that has an effect on the interaction possible is the **number of participants** involved. It is much easier to have lively discussion and brainstorming in a group of 4 than in a group of 25. The more participants joining the meeting, the more important it is to plan interactive sessions by using features that enable this, on whichever platform you are using. These might include polls, whiteboards, and virtual breakout rooms for group work.

In the graphic, you can see the varying levels of interaction required by specific types of group activity in virtual space.

LOW INTERACTION ──────────────────────────▶ **HIGH INTERACTION**

INFO SHARING

- Minimum amount of interaction
- It can be a purely informational meeting possibly with a presentation of facts, plans or conclusions from either one team member or a group of team members
- This can be followed by a discussion or Q&A session which would lead to a higher level of interaction

BRAINSTORMING & DECISION MAKING

- The collaborative element is more important
- The software should make it possible not only to share something but to interact – either writing or talking –, whilst discussing the diverse views which will need to be discussed

COLLABORATIVE WORK

- Generally based around idea generation of new concepts is the most challenging type of virtual meeting.
- Concrete examples are real features such as virtual whiteboards, collaborative writing tools with audio/video links can be great support.

When choosing the technology, it's also important that you remember to **use technologies that you feel comfortable with as a virtual facilitator**, and familiarise yourself with them before use. This advance preparation gives a sense of security to the team members and motivates them to use the tool but also allows you to foresee any potential problems, adjust any content or tasks accordingly, and promptly answer any questions participants may have when they start using the technology themselves.

Another important guideline is to not let technology take over your session. In other words, **keep the use of technology as simple as you can, and limit the number of technologies** used in one virtual meeting or training event. While it is tempting to use every new tool and feature, starting slowly will not only minimise the risk of technology 'glitches';
it will also help you to build up your experience and confidence. Using too many online components can not only be overwhelming; it may finally distract from the purpose
of the meeting.

CHAPTER 4 VIRTUAL MEETING FACILITATION

To summarise all of this, when you choose a technology tool for your online meeting, you will of course need to make sure that the tool chosen offers features that will enable you to achieve the meeting's purpose, and also that will offer the degree of interaction (or not) relevant to that purpose. However, it will also be of considerable help if you do some initial preparation in familiarising yourself with the possibilities of the selected tool and getting comfortable with it, at least to a level of technical competence where you can help meeting participant with any queries or challenges.

And try not to be too blinded by technology, as the saying goes – technological competence is of course important, but a good meetings facilitator can easily and quickly learn enough to cope with challenges without losing the flow of the session – calmness and a relaxed approach is more important than being a technical "whizz-kid".

Additionally, there are some further possible technological characteristics that might help your choice of technology when planning a virtual session. They range from basic and highly desirable, to not 100% essential for running a virtual session. We've listed some of these below, **clustered according to their category of usefulness.**

Basic technology characteristics that would be important for any kind of use (including web-meetings with lower levels of participation):

- Technology should be easy to use: user-friendly without too many buttons on the screen. This will allow all participants to overcome the "technological barrier"!
- Everybody should be able to see the same thing while working together online
- IM (instant messaging) and chat options (at least the chat option with the facilitator to ask questions, and also between participants) are very useful in stimulating discussion
- Voice and calling in options: the flexible option to call in via computer or phone
- Technology should make it easy to share and "co-create" documents, images, and so forth synchronously and visually on screen e.g. through file-sharing, screen and desktop-sharing options.

Additional characteristics you might consider as useful for interactive sessions (web-meetings, training etc.)

- **The Poll feature** – for voting on specific topics, and getting instant feedback from participants. A Poll is an online voting system on which web-meeting participants can choose between predefined answers to a question. The result of the poll voting can immediately be shared, and everyone gets a transparent view on the opinion of the whole group.

- **Break-out rooms:** the possibility offered by some technology platforms to work in smaller sub-groups in private online "breakout space" - on a specific topic/question, for example -and then to go back in the plenary to share ideas from whiteboards or slides that were noted in the breakout room/s.

- **Webcam option:** nice to have this but not an absolute 'must', depending on what it is being used to achieve. Seeing each other does help to break down virtual barriers but also requires a strong internet connection. And, in some cases, having constant visual contact can also be distracting, even undesirable – whether or not the internet connection is powerful enough to avoid technical problems.

- **Recording option.** The recording option is often used for information sharing sessions and training events where it might be useful to have the recorded version of the meeting available, for participants who didn't make it to the meeting or meeting participants who would like to take a second look.

Additional characteristics that are nice to have but not 100% necessary for a virtual session:

- The possibility to synchronise the tool with Outlook or other mail programmes

- Integration with other relevant tools

Remember that technology is just a means to an end. In other words, think about what you want to achieve, what your expected outcomes are - and then decide how any particular technology can support them, or not. You should also keep focused on your purpose: do not let technology features "distract" you from your work and what you actually want to get done.

CHAPTER 4 VIRTUAL MEETING FACILITATION

USEFUL TIPS BEFORE THE SESSION

You can probably find thousands of lists of 'tips' on the internet about virtual facilitation. Our goal in this chapter is to summarise some simple best practices that we have tried out ourselves and experienced first-hand that they work! In the field of virtual facilitation the company Nomadic has made huge steps in researching the most effective ways in facilitating a virtual session and we thank also Frederik Fogelberg and Jude Tavanyar[29] for their inspiration in compiling this list.

TUTORIAL/TRIAL SESSIONS ON HOW TO USE THE TECHNOLOGY

When using any technology tool, particularly for the first time, it is essential to make sure your participants feel comfortable with it and have the basic information they need to try it out. One quick way to achieve this is to send them a tutorial on how to use the tool prior to your meeting. You could also offer a short trial session (both individual and group session) on the tool for those who would rather experiment with it through a practice session first.

This is especially helpful when a team member has an active role in the meeting, for example when presenting one part of the session.

INVITE PEOPLE TO JOIN 10 MINUTES EARLIER THAN THE SESSION START

Asking participants to sign in 10 minutes earlier than the official start of the meeting gives people time to practice and get comfortable with the technology in use. This is especially helpful when you are signing in for the first time, as the computer usually has to download the software, and this might take several minutes.

During interactive sessions you could also use this 10 minutes before the start as a 'warm-up' and allow people to do fun exercises using the whiteboard or chat tools
(e.g. invite every participant to draw on the whiteboard what the weather is like where they are or share it in the Chat box).

---

29 F. Fogelberg, J. Tavanyar, et al "Live Connections: Virtual Facilitation for High Engagement and Powerful Learning", Nomadic, 2015

HAVE A "WORKPLACE CHECK" BEFORE STARTING THE SESSION

Here are some basic preparation points that are really useful to check before you start, as they will make all the differences to the smoothness of your session.

- No background noise (close windows if necessary, and "mute" any devices like a mobile phone)
- Good light and fresh air if at all possible
- Water or any other soft drink
- Reliable Internet connection
- Backup PC and phone line
- Professional and well-functioning headset
- Printed script and participant list
- No noisy household pets around, if working from home

CHAPTER 4 VIRTUAL MEETING FACILITATION

PREVENTING AND DEALING WITH PROBLEMS

Dealing with technology almost definitely means that you will have to face some difficult situations from time to time. Here are some ways to prevent them (taken from Nomadic IBP's training programme in "Virtual Facilitation Skills").

- **Technology check:** test the microphone beforehand, make sure the computer is functioning properly.

- **Workplace check:** close windows, check background noises, have a glass of water on the desk.

- **Use a wired Internet connection:** it provides better connection and is more secure than a wireless one.

- **Kick-off session to check technology:** make sure each participant is able to use the technology.

- **Ask participants to log-in a few minutes before** the official start of the session to check sound.

No matter how well you prepare beforehand in order to prevent problems arising, you are bound to encounter tricky situations occasionally which challenge your technical skills, and which may catch you out if you do not anticipate them and think about how you will react if or when they do come up.

HERE´S A LIST OF POSSIBLE THINGS THAT CAN HAPPEN:

- **The sound doesn't work:** people cannot hear you at all.
- **Microphone doesn't work properly:** people cannot understand you clearly.
- Participants are **not able to join the meeting** due to company firewalls, etc.
- **Sending the wrong link:** some participants still trying to join via the "old" link, even if you have sent an update link.
- **If you have closed a session by mistake:** you might not be able to restart the same session, and you´ll need to create a new one and send out a new link.
- Remember that sometimes the **chat can only be seen from the moment you have joined the meeting:** participants won't be able to read the chat history.
- **Before exiting** the meeting make sure to save the chat and the content, otherwise it gets lost.

Finally, how do you know if participants are giving their full attention or not?
Having participants doing e-mails or trying to work during your session – in other words, not really paying attention - could probably also be defined as "disaster", as it completely undermines the original purpose of having a virtual interaction.

There are different ways to find out whether participants are paying attention, like asking them to provide feedback on a topic, or answer questions - and see how long it takes. Depending on the system you are using there might be additional features you could use: e.g. as facilitator, you might also be able to see if participants' attention level is dropping as if they are looking into another computer program, their level of attention will automatically go down. Try to keep the meeting interactive, calling on people by name and asking for their comments and questions. The more you manage to create a dialogue and "real meeting" atmosphere, the more people will behave accordingly.

CHAPTER 4 VIRTUAL MEETING FACILITATION

4.2. ROLES AND FEATURES IN VIRTUAL MEETINGS
ROLES IN A VIRTUAL MEETING

When setting up a meeting it is also important to plan on "people issues" in terms of who will participate, who will be the presenter(s), who is in charge of the technology and who is in charge of documenting the meeting. The roles in a virtual meeting are similar to those in a face to face meeting, as suggested in the diagram:

ORGANISER/HOST

- Decides on the meeting, defines the goals, the purpose of the meeting and who should be participating.
- He/she can either facilitate the meeting him/herself or ask a second person to be the facilitator of the meeting

FACILITATOR

- This role can overlap with the organiser´s role but can also be done by a separate person.
- The facilitator is in charge of inviting the participants, preparing the agenda, sending out preparation material, coordinating with the presenter(s), time-keeping, thinking of different working formats, ensuring that all team members have a voice, documenting the Minutes to be sent out to all team members, and following up on feedback and next steps.

PRESENTER/SPEAKER

- The role of the presenter, which differs from the facilitator, is limited to — you guessed it — presenting during the meeting.
- Before the meeting the presenter will meet up with the facilitator also to make sure the technology is working properly (we advise a short trial session between facilitator and presenter). The presenter will usually be introduced by the facilitator, who will manage the interactions (e.g. Q&A) between audience and presenter. The presenter´s role is just to provide the presentation and to be responsible for the content. S/he is not usually responsible for the overall format/ structure of the whole session.

TECHNICAL MODERATOR

- The role of the technical moderator (sometimes called the 'producer') is key to the success of the virtual meeting. The technical moderator is responsible not only for setting up the meeting but also for making sure technologies work during the session.

- Knowing the tools very well, and being able to multi-task, are two important requirements when choosing the right technical moderator. That person will be responsible for answering any questions in the Chat box referring to technical problems, and should also be able to troubleshoot basic issues during the meeting.

VIRTUAL COACH

- The role of the virtual coach is to participate in the session, either incognito/as an observer or openly/officially, and to provide feedback to the facilitator and the presenter.

- The virtual coach has an observer role, looking at social dynamics, content and technical set-up. The virtual coach can also provide "live-feedback" via chat during the session to the facilitator or written feedback later about the content and impression made by the facilitator during the session. The virtual coach role is not always necessary, but can be extremely useful for improving facilitator's delivery in future sessions.

PARTICIPANTS

- Participants are requested to engage in the preparation process by handing in their agenda topics and preparation material, and also by actively engaging in discussions and in decision-making.

- We note from experience that it can be very useful to have a starter question which engages all members of the group at the beginning of the session, and requires each member to answer. This type of question helps everyone to feel involved at once, and also builds people's confidence in contributing to discussion of the meeting's agenda.

CHAPTER 4 VIRTUAL MEETING FACILITATION

VIRTUAL FEATURES

When designing a virtual session you have to distinguish between **"features"**, which are basically tools that enable virtual interaction, and **"interventions"** or ways of working, which are the approaches and activities you use as a virtual facilitator to allow collaboration and social interaction.

On the right you can find a list of some common features used during virtual session with some explanation.

We can compare the "features" to the "room setting" when thinking about a face-to-face meeting. They are of course a vital element for virtual meetings. Interventions define how people interact with each other during the virtual meeting and are important key element to a successful virtual interaction. (Source: Nomadic training "Virtual Facilitation Skills")

In the next part of the chapter you will find some tips on how to use the features of web meeting tools and how to design virtual meetings by using the right interventions.

FEATURES	DESCRIPTION
Audio	It can be used via computer (headset/mic) or dialing in via telephone.
Screen sharing	Allows the participants to see your screen and to share somebody elses screen. Can be also challenging for privacy issues … Alternative is to upload the document you want to share and show it online.
Annotation tools	Writing, drawing, etc. can be done on the slides and be saved for future use.
Chat	Adds interactivity and engagement, possibility to chat to all participants at the same time or to have private chats.
Recording	Possibility to record the session for later use.
Icóns	Visible at the side bar, next to participant's names - to communicate without interrupting (icons are not available for all kind of software), e.g. raise hand.
Whiteboard	"Free writing on the screen" - good for brainstorming and generating ideas or socializing/warm up. For writing and drawing.
Breakout rooms	Possibility to split the group into sub-groups for more effective working sessions. Excellent for developing ideas and discussing.
Polls	People can vote and the results can be shown immediately.
Surveys	Cannot show results immediately, like a poll. Good for evaluation before or after the session.
Quizzes and tests	Link to website, where participants can answer questions (e.g. , multiple-choice questions) e.g. http://www.guia.com/web.
Application sharing	Possibility, also for the participants, to share one PPT, Word document or single pictures.

Fig. 14: Source: Nomadic training "Virtual Facilitation Skills"

CHAPTER 4 VIRTUAL MEETING FACILITATION

4.3. VIRTUAL MEETINGS IN PRACTICE

As you will by now be aware, there is a great deal of theory, and checklists of tips and best practices on how to facilitate virtual meetings successfully. However, "one size does not fit all", and trial and error is a good rule here – we found that the best way for us as change management consultants was to just try out different approaches in our current projects and combine that experiential learning with the knowledge we have already gained from running effective and productive meetings face to face. Indeed, we realized that most of the things that prove to be successful in face to face meetings could also be easily adapted in virtual meetings – it just needed some creativity and knowledge to "translate" into the virtual context.

In the next section of this book you will find both practical checklists and stories drawn from our experience of applying these. Above all, we hope that you get inspired to try something new in your next virtual meeting with your team colleagues, customers, suppliers or other partners.

HOW TO AVOID "MEETING TOURISM" SYNDROME

A lot of managers complain about what is often known as **"meeting tourism syndrome"** – in other words, rushing from one meeting to the other at top speed with little time to prepare for any of them. And, when that happens, here below are some examples of what can often happen at the same time. If you recognise any of this (somewhat nightmarish scenario), you may be suffering from "meeting tourism syndrome"!

- You enter a meeting where there is no agenda and you find out that you and half your colleagues who are attending the meeting have no active role and would have been better off by receiving the information via email.

- As a consequence you might follow the discussion with one ear, check your mails on your smartphone, or drift into a daydream about how else you could use the time you are wasting right now. Whatever you are doing, you are probably not paying attention to what is happening in the meeting.

- Then, checking your calendar rather than listening/participating, you start freaking out because you realize that you might have to do another evening shift at work, simply because you have so much work on your desk and no time to do it as your calendar is full of meetings. Meetings like this one.

- You end up leaving the meeting with a full head of looping, circular discussions, which appeared to have achieved no results. And you don't even have the time to reflect on what just happened, or complain about the waste of your valuable time, because you are already late for your next meeting, which started 10 minutes ago.

If this sounds like an all-too-familiar sequence of events in your working day, and one which you would like to avoid in future, there is hope! You can certainly find ways to prevent your virtual meetings taking shape in the same way. On the next pages you will find some rules of thumb for meetings preparation which are valid for any virtual and face to face meetings that you need to organise and run.

In the virtual context, additional considerations do come into play as participants of the meetings can obviously get distracted and end up doing completely different things while being in the meeting – without anyone noticing, including you. There are so many distractions on offer, and here are some of the more common ones, according to the Harvard Business Review[30].

30 Harvard Business Review, Gretchen Gavett, What People are Really Doing When They're on a Conference Call, August 2014.

CHAPTER 4 VIRTUAL MEETING FACILITATION

Virtual meetings always follow a certain process. We call it the "meeting facilitation loop". A good meeting starts with the right preparation. Once the meeting starts, there is an introduction part where participants get involved and ready for the joint work. We call this part of the meeting the "warm up". During the meeting there are different aspects that a virtual meeting facilitator should consider –namely "the four dimensions" of content (what should be discussed), time (when and how long), space (where and in which format using which tool) and social dimension (who with whom). An effective meeting usually ends with a wrap up phase consisting of joint action orientation on decisions made and tasks assigned. A meeting can be efficient and fun but it will be without impact if there is no follow up on the implementation. The follow up is also sometimes part of the preparation for the next meeting… and another "meeting facilitation loop" begins.

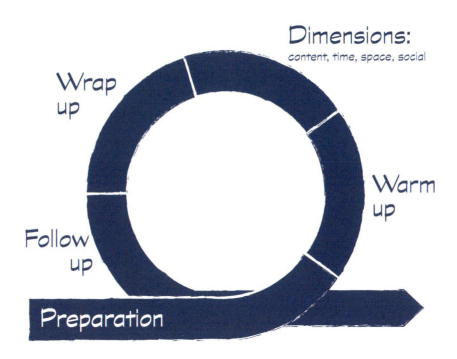

Fig. 15: Meeting facilitation loop © Doujak Corporate Development

CHAPTER 4 VIRTUAL MEETING FACILITATION

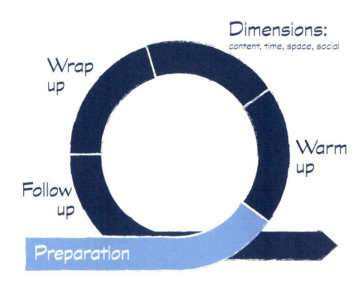

PREPARATION – DESIGNING THE VIRTUAL MEETING

A good meeting starts with the right preparation.

THE MAIN GOALS OF GOOD MEETING PREPARATION ARE TO:

Clarify upfront what you want to achieve (define the meeting objectives).

Define what is expected from each participant/his or her 'role' at the meeting.

Enable/support all participants in fulfilling their roles –
preparing effectively for what they need to achieve individually.

And the very first questions to ask are these – Why is this meeting taking place? Do I really need to hold the meeting? What do I want to achieve? And if the meeting should go ahead, who needs to participate in it? The diagrammes from Elizabeth Grace Saunders provide a 'mind map' to look at different stages and options in answering some of these questions.

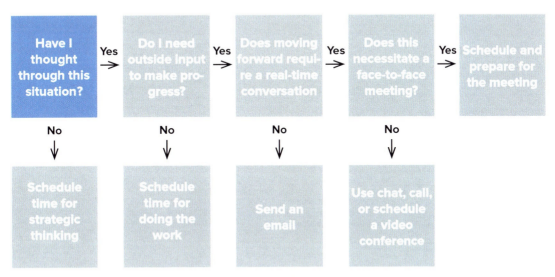

SOURCE: REAL LIFE E TIME COACHING & TRAINING HBR.ORG

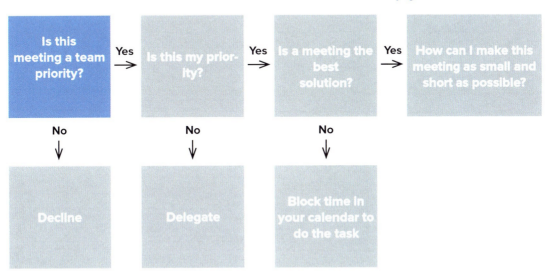

31 Harvard Business Review, Elizabeth Grace Saunders, Do You Really Need to Hold That Meeting? March 2015.

CHAPTER 4 VIRTUAL MEETING FACILITATION

BEFORE SENDING OUT A VIRTUAL MEETING INVITATION YOU SHOULD THINK OF THE FOLLOWING QUESTIONS:

CHECKLIST

- ☑ Goal: What is the purpose of the meeting? (content, social, emotional, process)
- ☑ Necessity: Do I really need this meeting?
- ☑ Participants: Who are the participants? How big is the group? What is their experience with technology and how much interactivity can they cope with? Are the participants joining the meeting continuously or only sequentially as guests?
- ☑ Priorities: What are the key focus points? (content /social)
- ☑ Agenda: What is the agenda /storyboard /script?
- ☑ Roles: How can the structure and the role-sharing be clearly defined? (Sharing of roles between participant, organizer, facilitator, speaker, technical moderator, person guiding the protocol, communications team, observers, coaches, etc.)
- ☑ Activation: How can we 'activate' the participants and keep them engaged?
- ☑ Preparation: What are the preparatory tasks, observation tasks, work-related tasks, documents and symbols they should be familiar with, etc.? What are the virtual features required?
- ☑ Diagnosis: Do we understand the interests of the various parties? What are the preliminary results, hypotheses on the overall situation?
- ☑ Infrastructure: What else needs to be organized? (Web meeting invitation, setting up polls, getting the right equipment such as headset or camera etc.)
- ☑ Decision-making: are there important things that need to be decided? How will the decision making process be set up? (Do we all need to agree? Is it enough if the majority agrees? Or do I as team leader want to decide, and just ask for some ideas and feedback from the participants?)

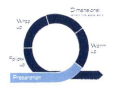

PRACTICAL FACILITATION TIPS FOR THE PREPARATION

Planning is already half of the work

- Take sufficient time for planning the meeting. This will save both your time, and that of your colleagues, and generally increase efficiency. Our tip: plan at least half the time for planning as for the meeting itself – meaning that you should invest 1 hour preparation for a 3 hour meeting.

- Provide an agenda well in advance including the goal of each agenda item, required time, required communication channel and any preparation work required by participants.

- Structure the agenda so that everyone has the opportunity to contribute.

- Take time to define in advance how much "speaking time" or "airtime" is needed by anyone presenting or speaking at your web meeting, and also plan sufficient time for discussion.

- Plan sufficient time to provide "think breaks", especially if there are non-native speakers present.

Share information upfront: Provide information about where to find the relevant documents e.g. a shared database, a server-based system such as SharePoint, or virtual team space. Make sure that you have the results of previous decisions, and an up-to-date "to do" list available.

Use the technology well: Get familiar with the technology in advance of the meeting, and plan how to use features such as using webcam, chat box, polls, whiteboards, video clips or other features.

Rotation of the facilitator role: Make sure that other team members also learn how to facilitate virtual meetings. This not only helps to share the workload, it also increases understanding in general about what makes virtual meetings "special and different", and so helps to establish a collaborative approach and "culture" of ideas about what makes virtual meetings productive.

CHAPTER 4 VIRTUAL MEETING FACILITATION

Preparation tasks: Actively involve meeting participants before and during the meeting by assigning preparation tasks.

When registering for the meeting, ask participants to fill out some questions regarding their opinions about the different agenda items/questions - you could even ask them for their expectations of the meeting itself. For each agenda item you would then have a consolidated, perhaps anonymised picture of what team members expect as outcomes for each item, and thus a clear basis for discussion.

Roles in the meeting: Assign roles such as technical moderator, time keeper, observer, minute-taker etc. This makes people more attentive during the meeting and enables the facilitator to fully focus on running the meeting itself.

For 'sequential meeting' participation: Structure the agenda so that people can come in and out of meetings according to their needs for information input.

Meeting rules: Establish collaborative "rules" for setting up and participating in meetings. These might include points such as:

- The deadline for sending out an agenda and preparation tasks (3 days in advance)
- The deadline for sending out documentation after the meeting (1 day after the meeting)
- Everyone logs in 5 -10 minutes before the meeting to test technology
- Everyone has responsibility for punctuality to ensure the meeting can start on time without technical trouble shooting.

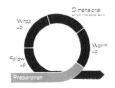

CASE EXAMPLE: INCREASING MEETING EFFICIENCY

One of our clients needed to improve their meeting efficiency and get rid of 'alignment' meetings that were taking up, and apparently wasting, valuable executive time. They therefore decided to make an assessment of the current meeting structure (including virtual meetings as well as face to face ones), placing a particular emphasis on identifying goals, meeting topics and required participants.

The result was that the way in which meetings were structured, and took place, was completely transformed. Here are a few of the highlights.

- Rules for meetings, and standards for running these were established for the entire organisation.
- Some regular meetings such as 'jour fixes' or 'alignment rounds' got cancelled, as people realized that there was no further need for them.
- Other regular meetings got modified from a weekly face to face meeting into a biweekly web meeting as it was realised that there was no necessity to meet in person.
- Other meetings again were scaled down significantly in size, reducing the number of required participants from 20 to 5. Those who no longer needed to attend certain meetings were kept informed via the meeting Minutes.

One of the most significant changes that this 'restructuring' of a meeting process involved was establishing an important distinction between **'ad hoc'** meetings and **'regular'** meetings. Ad hoc meetings are spontaneous ones which are often set to enable alignment on small tactical operative topics, or crisis meetings in case of an emergency. These meetings are rather short, to the point and don't require an agenda upfront.

All other ('regular') meetings require an agenda, with goals for each specific agenda item and roles for participants with tasks relating to them. They also require prompt minutes to be issued post-meeting with a clear 'to do' list.

The effect of all this change was surprisingly impactful.

- People simply didn't join regular meetings if they had not received an agenda upfront.
- The change of meeting culture resulted in better prepared and discussed decisions which had a positive impact on the company's development.
- Unfortunately we haven't measured the exact amount of effective executive time saved from useless meetings and travel but we know that it freed up capacity considerably for new innovative projects.

CHAPTER 4 VIRTUAL MEETING FACILITATION

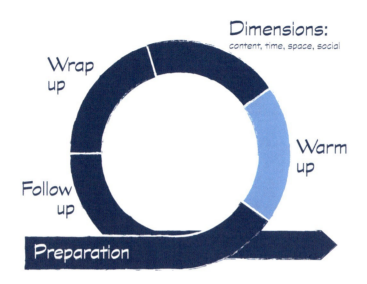

WARM UP

I am sure you have already experienced the situation that you are in a call or web meeting and the facilitator asks a question and all he gets in return is an extended silence. If you have, please accept our commiserations. But why does this happen? It could be, on the one hand, because participants are not 100% attentive at that moment, and are checking their mails or doing something else that does not relate to the meeting in any way. Of course, this is not ideal and we hope that by now in reading this book you have some sound practical ideas to keep participants' engagement in your meeting.

However, the other reason why a meeting facilitator hears silence might be because participants are simply not sure how, when (or even whether) to contribute. In other words, the "virtual ice" has not yet been broken. Therefore it is advisable when planning and preparing a virtual meeting to actively plan interactive sessions right from the start, ideally within the first 2 minutes. We call this kind of involvement a "warm up".

GOALS FOR THE 'WARM UP':

Create a positive working environment

Show how collaborative work can happen in virtual meetings

Draw attention to the difference between the individual and the group – have some activity where every single meeting participant can join the meeting and at the same time create a meeting spirit so that the "group" of participants can be formed.

CHECKLIST: WHEN STARTING THE MEETING:

- ☑ Welcome each participant by name when joining the session
- ☑ Have them say something aloud, to check the quality of their microphone and that everything works
- ☑ If you are planning an interactive session, have everybody "unmuted". On the other hand, if you are planning a webinar (online seminar) with a bigger audience, it is re-commended to keep everybody muted and "unmute" single participants when needed

CHAPTER 4 VIRTUAL MEETING FACILITATION

TIPS: WHAT TO DO AS A WARM UP:

Depending on the purpose and content of the meeting, warm ups can be used in different ways and can have different qualities. On the next pages you will find tips **WHAT** to do as a warm up and **HOW** to do it – taking advantage of virtual meeting features.

Informal 'tuning in' to each other:

Taking advantage of the waiting time until everyone has joined the meeting for some chat and personal talk might help to 'warm people up' and get them connected. A chat about the current weather in each country or the weekend plans gets people closer together and has a similar effect as the coffee break talks in face to face meetings. (If your team is meeting regularly in virtual space, take care to vary the topics a bit!)

Warm up examples:

- *"Hello everyone, what is the weather in your country at the moment? Here in Vienna it is snowing right now…"*
- *"What are your plans for the weekend?"*
- *"Have you made your plans for summer holidays already?"*

Getting to know each other:

If participants in the meeting don't know each other yet, it is advisable to start with a quick introduction round to "break the ice". We often use a template with key questions which everyone answers. This gives everyone a little bit of structure as to how to introduce themselves, and ensures that speaking time is equally distributed.

Warm up examples:

Please introduce yourself briefly, mentioning your: Professional background, current position, country you work in.

"Mood check":

A quick "mood check" – on the current mood in the department, or the individual mood and energy level of the meeting participants - gets everybody on board and also gives you additional information on how to understand where the people in your meeting are coming from emotionally – valuable information for "reading between the lines" on what is said.

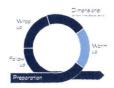

Warm up examples:

- *How are you today?*
- *If you had to describe the mood in your department/region/country as a kind of weather, what would you say the "weather" is like today?*

"Status check":

Getting crucial information on the current situation of a project/department or organisation right from the start makes it easier to focus the discussion on the essential topics. Therefore a general status check at the beginning of the meeting might be advisable.

Warm up examples:

- *Short update: What has kept you busy over the last month?*
  Change being in the air, how would you describe the "change weather" in your unit at the moment?
- *How would you describe the current situation in your project/market in an image or photo? Prepare for 2 minutes and then we'll start.*

"Expectation check":

Asking participants about their expectations for the meeting or special topics on the agenda might help to sharpen the focus of the meeting and get everyone thinking about what is essential to them.

Warm up examples:

- *What are your expectations /hopes for this meeting?*
- *What would be a good result from this meeting for your department?*
- *Which of the 3 topics on the agenda is the most relevant for you, and why?*
- *What are the biggest challenges? What should we pay attention to?*

CHAPTER 4 VIRTUAL MEETING FACILITATION

TIPS: WHAT TO DO AS WARM UP

TAKE INTO CONSIDERATION:

"Shaking up" or "Providing security":

A warm up can also have the function of "provoking" or "shaking people up" in order to get everybody focused on the work ahead. Sometimes a surprising question or quote like a critical statement of a newspaper headline can quickly get the attention and focus of everyone in the virtual meeting room. In times of change, it might be advisable to start with something reassuring, which provides security and takes away any fears and rumours that are lingering in people's minds right from the beginning.

Warm up examples:
For *providing security:* What do we know about the current market situation? Let's put together what we have collected and get a joint picture on the status (etc)
For *shaking up:* If we continue in this direction, how many months will our company still be alive?

Take into consideration the temporal dynamics of "acceleration" vs. "deceleration":

- Do you have the impression that everyone is stressed and rushing from meeting to meeting? If it's possible that they might want to slow down a bit when they arrive in the room, think about running a 'warm up' activity which **decelerates** people rather than accelerates the speed at which things are done. A good example could be a 5 minute individual reflection on the main topic on the agenda. Just asking people to sit quietly and think, gathering their thoughts and ideas for a few minutes before the discussion beings.

- Do you have an early morning or late evening meeting and everyone is tired? Then you might need something to 'speed things up' and get people in an **accelerated** working mode. A useful activity might be a quick round where everyone has only 1 minute to state their point on a certain topic. While people are giving their statement, a countdown clock shows on the screen. This exercise helps participants to focus on the essentials and also gives them time pressure – all of which will definitely wake them up!

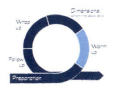

TIPS: HOW TO DO THE WARM UP
SOME FEATURES WHICH CAN HELP YOU RUN A 'VIRTUAL WARM UP'

... using the chat box:

Best to use for informal chats before the official meeting starts or if there is a high number of meeting participants.

Warm up examples:

- "How to accelerate sales is the key question for this meeting on the screen right now- please write down the 2-3 first ideas that come into your mind"
- "Having our yearly kick off meeting today. Please use the chat box for writing down one word/statement which represents your goal for 2016 best" or "What's your personal motto for 2016?"

... using a poll:

Polls are good methods to get a quick 'temperature check' of the mood in the group, and also to enable anonymous feedback.

Warm up examples:

- *How comfortable do you feel at the moment using virtual tools for collaboration?*
  1 = Feeling great!
  2= I do it sometimes, but I don't feel 100% comfortable,
  3= Feeling uncomfortable still, but ready to learn,
  4= I'm not interested, it is too complicated anyway
- *Which of the three topics on the agenda is most relevant for me?*
- *What's the workload in your department at the moment?*
  1= more than 100% – I am totally overloaded
  2= between 100 and 75% – it is quite a lot of work, but I would actually take on some new things
  3= 75%-50% – it's quite a lot of work, but I could actually take on some new things
  4= 50%-0 – currently I don't have much to do, desperately waiting for a new project to start

CHAPTER 4 VIRTUAL MEETING FACILITATION

TIPS: HOW TO DO THE WARM UP

… personally addressing each participant:

Facilitating virtually requires a bit more effort from the facilitator in terms of engaging each person and keeping them feeling comfortable and involved. This is for a variety of reasons, as discussed throughout this book, but one of the key ones is that as participants sometimes don't see each other (when webcams are not used) they just don't know who will get to speak when. So being clear about the process you are following as facilitator, in order to highlight when people can expect to be asked for comments, is highly advisable. Of course, you may not want do to this all the time, as it's a very structured approach and sometimes can take up a lot of time. But it does help to keep people engaged when you need to hear everyone's thoughts and ideas.

Warm up example:

- *A statement from everyone in the meeting on this topic please, starting with the participants list from the top to the bottom- we'll start with xxx*
- *A statement from everyone please, going country by country – let's start with the Chinese colleagues then going to the US,… and finally ending in Europe….*
- *A statement from everyone please, let's start with Mr X, when you have finished you can choose to whom you want to hand over.*

… by using the whiteboard and annotation function:

With experienced groups, one of my favourite warm up methods is to use the whiteboard function (if provided by the virtual meeting platform). This function enables everyone to write down statements and ideas at the same time. These can then be clustered together just like on a normal whiteboard.

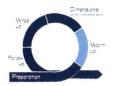

In order to get the described warm up options and their possible impact more tangible, we have included some case examples.

WARM UP CASE EXAMLE 1: MOOD CHECK WITH SMILEYS

For one meeting I uploaded this picture of the different emoticon 'smileys' and asked everyone to use the annotation function and place an arrow with their name in it on the relevant smiley (and of course you could also ask everyone to choose one smiley, say which one it was and you mark it for them). The result was quite diverse. A lot of participants were in the "smiling"-section of the smileys but there were also two people who chose the crying and negative smiley. Both stated that their mood had nothing to do with this meeting but with the current situation in their market and explained the context a bit.

This helped in two ways. Firstly, it provided very interesting and useful information for everyone in the meeting because they got a hint on what was going on in the other markets. Secondly, it also helped me as facilitator to differentiate between the "general bad mood" that was present during the meeting, and which had nothing to do with the topic we were discussing - and the real criticism, which was addressed to the other topics on the agenda.

CHAPTER 4 VIRTUAL MEETING FACILITATION

MOOD CHECK: OTHER EXAMPLES

"Weather mood check":

Similar to the smileys, the mood check can also be done with pictures of different types of weather. The question can be used in relation to personal mood but also when asking about the mood in a specific department or country.

Energy level:

For the 'energy level warm up', either a poll or the annotation function can be used, so that people can indicate how high their energy level is. You could then discuss what they would need in order to lift their energy again.

How is your energy level?

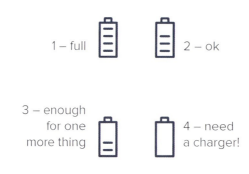

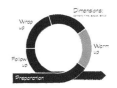

WARM UP CASE EXAMPLE 2: HOW TO MANAGE RESISTANCE FOR A NEW PROJECT?

It was right before Christmas and the management team wanted to launch a new project. During the preparation for the meeting the team leader and I talked about how currently most team members are already doing night and weekend shifts and are desperately looking forward to their Christmas holidays. So, coming up with this new project would cause a lot of resistance and stress. We discussed the option of postponing the "kick off" web meeting date to after Christmas, but due to management priorities it was decided that it had to happen right before.

So we decided to address the capacity topic right from the beginning. We started the meeting with a poll asking everyone to state their current work load level and comment on it.

What's your work load at the moment?

- 1= more than 100% – I am totally overloaded, can't wait for Christmas to come!
- 2= between 100 and 75% – quite some things to do and I am fighting but it is manageable
- 3= 75-50% – it's quite a lot of work, but I could actually take on some new things
- 4= 50-0 – currently I don't have much to do, desperately waiting for a new project to start

The result was the following:

- 1= 70% of the answers
- 2= 20% of the answers
- 3= 10% of the answers
- 4= 0% of the answers

CHAPTER 4 VIRTUAL MEETING FACILITATION

WARM UP CASE EXAMPLE 2: HOW TO MANAGE RESISTANCE FOR A NEW PROJECT?

Our assumptions were just reflected in the poll results. The comments were around:

- "There are too many things happening at the same time, I could work 24/7"
- "There are no clear priorities, everything is urgent all the time"
- "I have no feeling of success at all because every time I finish something I realise that there are three new things that just came in"

We ended up discussing for 60 minutes about how to prioritize the current work load for everyone. It became evident that it needed some management of stakeholder expectations and some more prioritisation work by the team leader. We also discovered that actually 20% of the participants managed to do their work and were also willing to support the others regarding best practices on how to do so. During the discussion we realized that for most team members there was an issue about managing the personal ambition of making everything perfect and finishing everything on time. So we also worked on how to see just small tasks that were accomplished as 'little successes', and ones which also deserve to be honoured. In doing this, we also discovered that 10% of the team members actually had capacity to either support people who were overloaded or take on new tasks themselves.

After this fairly intense discussion and some defined tasks on how to tackle the emerging issues, we finally spent the last 15 minutes of the meeting in introducing the new project. The effect was very interesting! Instead of resisting and telling us why this new thing wouldn't work, all team members were able to discuss and get used to the new project with a lot of focus and interest. Why was this? We consider it is because the full exploration and consideration given to everyone's workload constraints had enabled people to feel supported, and that their work load issue would be solved somehow. As a result, they had the energy and a fresher mind for the new project coming up ahead.

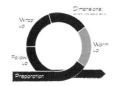

CASE EXAMPLE 3: VISUALIZING THE CHALLENGES AND ADVANTAGES OF THE DIFFERENT STAGES IN A CHANGE PROJECT, AND EXCHANGING BEST PRACTICES

Rolling out a new IT system is always connected to a lot of challenges and it is very likely that, even though you try to think of everything during the preparation phase, as soon as the system goes 'live', things still do not work smoothly due to new processes that still need to be streamlined, problems with data quality or other challenges that are popping up.

In this best practice story, an international industrial company was in the middle of the roll-out of a new ERP (enterprise resource planning) system, followed by new processes and structures. We had established monthly webinars for the project community, consisting of representatives from each country and from different functions, who would report current challenges and (hopefully also) share best practices.

The roll out was done sequentially – in the US, which was the pilot market, the "go live" of the new system had already been implemented for a few months and worked almost smoothly, whereas in the Central and Eastern Europe region, two weeks after the "go live", there were complaints about "a disaster" with "nothing working at all" and "a lot of customer complaints threatening to leave to the competition if this is not solved instantly". Having heard all that, the Spanish and Italian colleagues who were just about to prepare for the "go live" taking place in a few months' time got really nervous.

In general, you can imagine that we were expecting a lot of explosive material in this monthly, 90 minutes web meeting. So what can a warm up activity do in this case in order to calm down and get people into a productive working mode? We started the web meeting with a picture of different roads and asked the participants to tell us "where their country is currently on our journey"?

We intentionally asked the US colleagues to start. Luckily they chose the picture of the bright and modern road, enabling them to drive smoothly into the future. They reflected that it had not always been that way – just a few months ago the road was bumpy with some holes in it, but working together with the project team they managed to pass by the bumps and holes, and now were really able to see the benefit of the journey they had made.

CHAPTER 4 VIRTUAL MEETING FACILITATION

CASE EXAMPLE 3: VISUALIZING THE CHALLENGES AND ADVANTAGES OF THE DIFFERENT STAGES IN A CHANGE PROJECT, AND EXCHANGING BEST PRACTICES

We intentionally asked the US colleagues to start. Luckily they chose the picture of the bright and modern road, enabling them to drive smoothly into the future. They reflected that it had not always been that way – just a few months ago the road was bumpy with some holes in it, but working together with the project team they managed to pass by the bumps and holes, and now were really able to see the benefit of the journey they had made.

The CEE colleagues chose the worst road you could imagine with traffic jams, big holes and horrible weather conditions. The Spanish and Italian colleagues said that they currently couldn't see the road due to dust, and that they were hearing on the news from the car radio about the conditions in CEE which made them reluctant to continue driving on that path!

So here we were. That was the current situation, in a metaphor. Everything was on the table – so how to work with that? During the web meeting we tried to work out together what actually helped the US colleagues to enter the modern new road and how these learnings could be transferred to the CEE situation. From the current CEE situation we tried to collect factors which could have been prevented or managed differently in the "go live" preparation phase, which in turn was really helpful for the Spanish and Italian team.

In the end, the atmosphere in the meeting was very productive. Some key points were discussed and explored in depth, leading to additional two-way 'coaching web meetings' between the US and CEE colleagues, to explore past mistakes and good practice, and learn from both.

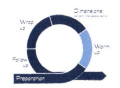

WHAT IS THE CURRENT SITUATION IN YOUR PROJECT/MARKET?

CHAPTER 4 VIRTUAL MEETING FACILITATION

WARM UPS are a very powerful activity and sometimes identify key points that define the mood, work flow and focus of the web meeting right from the beginning. They can be short, with one statement by each participant, or a stimulus for longer discussions.

How you use them depends on what you want to achieve in the meeting and how you assess the situation of your meeting participants. From our experience, it can make a huge difference whether there is a warm up activity within a meeting, or not. Why not try it out and see what happens!

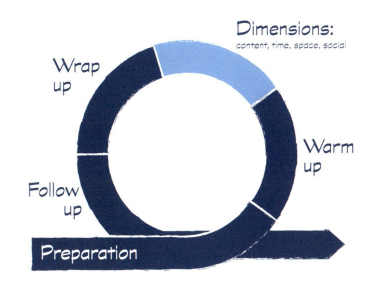

> **We have defined four dimensions which influence virtual meetings: Content, Time, Space, And Social**

CHAPTER 4 VIRTUAL MEETING FACILITATION

THE CONTENT, TIME, SPACE AND SOCIAL DIMENSION

So far we have talked about how you prepare the meeting and start it off with a good warm up session, so that everyone is focused and active. Now it is time to discuss the overall structure of the meeting and see how you might design the different sequences.

We have defined **four dimensions which influence virtual meetings:**

- Content (what)

- Time (when, how long)

- Space (where, and in which format, with which tool)

- Social (who, with whom)

The **content dimension** deals with WHAT you want to communicate and WHICH format would be the most effective way to do so. The **time dimension** refers to effective time management in the sense of "achieving the goal" in the web meeting, and how much time the meeting therefore requires. The **spatial dimension** is connected to the right selection of the web meeting format or tool – from the web meeting system itself right through to the different features within it, such as screen-sharing, video, poll, annotation functions, whiteboard, chat, etc. The **social dimension** combines the content-related goal with the social process, taking group dynamics into account and taking advantage of team collaboration.

CONTENT DIMENSION

GOAL:

Understand, accept and effectively communicate the content

CHECKLIST CONTENT DIMENSION

- ☑ First things first, Management Summary
- ☑ Limit the number of slides
- ☑ Limit the information on each slide and use 'emotional'/evocative pictures if possible.
- ☑ Make sure that you have a regular movement of the image you display (moving to the next slide every 1-2- minutes)
- ☑ Standardization of reports and draft decisions: e.g. Context, objectives, projections and assumptions, hypotheses of the current situation, suggested proposals /decisions (possibly including own ratings), further steps, and so on
- ☑ Time: Deal with limited time by working productively and efficiently with priority issues

CHAPTER 4 VIRTUAL MEETING FACILITATION

PRACTICAL FACILITATION TIPS:

Before sending out a virtual meeting invitation you should think of the following questions:

- **Define the outcome:** The content dimension refers to the message which you would like to transmit and the result you would like to achieve. The task of the facilitator is to clarify the objectives of the content's message, and to think of how it should be conveyed to others. Is it a topic which requires a short input in the form of an updated presentation, is it a discussion point or is it a decision making session where you need to end up with a joint agreement and defined tasks regarding how to proceed? Depending on the answer to these questions above, the meeting will of course vary significantly in its set-up.

- **Plan discussion sessions:** In case there is input in the form of a presentation it is advisable to think of discussion questions in advance, in order to ensure that the discussion goes in the right direction and everyone in the meeting knows how to contribute fully.

- **Think of a range of ways of conveying information:** Instead of a PowerPoint or Excel presentation, an interview setting could be something very refreshing and might capture people's attention more than the traditional 'monologue-style' speech, for example. A good combination of presentation/input and discussion also can be structured by actively promoting questions from people. I find it useful sometimes to collect questions before the presentation so that the person leading it knows what to focus on, and the kinds of topics participants want to know more about.

- **Less is sometimes more, regarding content:** A key question for the meetings facilitator is – how to balance text content and visuals? For information sessions in a web meeting, we find that it can often be a great idea to use slides as a "story telling" function, to help you and others "visualise" or envisage in their mind's eye what you are talking about. We recommend using big pictures that have an impact on the audience to get their attention, and to limit any text to one message per slide. Your brain can process images must faster than it can process words. Psychologists also talk about the superiority effect which refers to the notion that concepts that are learned by viewing pictures are more easily and frequently recalled than are concepts that are learned by viewing their written word form counterparts.[32] And of course, detailed PowerPoint presentations and any other handouts can still be sent before/after the meeting.

32 https://en.wikipedia.org/wiki/Picture_superiority_effect

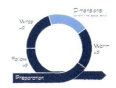

TIME DIMENSION
GOAL:
Effective time management in the sense of "achieving the goal".

Time is always a very sensitive issue in web meetings, and being over-optimistic regarding how much content and discussion can be fitted into a short meeting has a detrimental impact upon everyone. Virtual meetings can be even more exhausting than personal meetings for all concerned, and often take up more energy than we imagine. The timeline of your meeting needs to be well-managed and realistic, and so to avoid over-planning, and draining the engagement and goodwill of your participants (and yourself), we have developed some useful 'rules of thumb' regarding time and timing in virtual meetings.

CHECKLIST TIME DIMENSION

Rules of thumb/appropriate timings for virtual meetings:

- ⌛ 15 seconds: Individual work ("Before we start, please briefly reflect on your experiences relating to this topic")
- ⌛ 30 seconds: Short feedback from each participant/per person
- ⌛ 1 minute: Personal introduction per person 'in the round' – or for a short report
- ⌛ 1 minute: Average duration per slide in case of a presentation
- ⌛ 2 minutes: Small discussion groups at the beginning* (*make sure you have virtual break out rooms such as parallel meeting sessions or messaging services available)
- ⌛ 5–10 minutes: Welcome, explanation of initial situation and definition of goals
- ⌛ 5–7 minutes: Presentation: status update of a project
- ⌛ 10 minutes: Minimum group discussion involving 3 member-groups (group work: 20-90 min.)
- ⌛ 5-10 minutes: Short break in a web meeting
- ⌛ 20 minutes: Maximum time for any single presentation
- ⌛ 60-90 minutes: ideal duration time for any web meeting
- ⌛ 3 hours: absolute maximum duration of a web meeting, including 2 breaks in between

CHAPTER 4 VIRTUAL MEETING FACILITATION

PRACTICAL FACILITATION TIPS:

We would recommend taking into consideration the following points:

- **90 minutes rule:** A web meeting should ideally not last longer than 90 minutes. In case it takes longer, plan breaks after 60 minutes. Meetings longer than 90 minutes already start to take on the flavour of a workshop, and if it is such, you need to consider running simultaneous working sessions in break out rooms so that people can talk in small groups for maximum engagement.

- **Breaks:** Do not forget to build in a coffee break if you are planning a session longer than 60 to max 90 minutes. For example: use a timer that every participant could see on their screen and set up 5 minutes break to allow participants to stretch their legs, make a coffee or go to the loo. A nice online tool we use is the online stopwatch.[33]

- **Plan the agenda exactly to within a 5 minutes 'margin of error' and, within that, allocate time for giving feedback:** This way of planning also includes planning of time for discussion and interactive formats such as Polls.

- **Maintain time discipline – start on time.**

- **Appoint a time-keeper:** The role of the time keeper is an easy task which enables the facilitator to focus solely on the process of leading the session or meeting.

- **Consider the "rhythm" of the meeting:** Where do we have to be slow, where can we go quickly? In the warm up part we already discussed that for some topics it might be important to slow down to get everyone's attention and focus. For other topics which can sometimes lead to rather rambling discussions, it might be more advisable to speed up and get the topic voted on quickly. Only you and your meeting participants will know which is which!

- **Balance between exchange of short points and 'deep themes':** After a long discussion point which finally reached a consensus, a short and crisp topic which can be solved quickly energises people, because a quick gain or result can be identified. Therefore it sometimes can be helpful to apply the "sandwich method" of energy management: a long, then a short and then a long topic again.

- **Be fair with time zones:** When operating in different time zones make sure to share the load of late night or early morning sessions. There is no one more demotivated than the team member who regularly has to get up in the middle of their night to attend your daytime meeting, and no one offers to take the burden from them.

---

33 http://www.online-stopwatch.com/full-screen-online-countdown

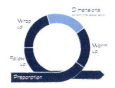

SPATIAL DIMENSION:

GOAL:

Choosing the right system and features for the right purpose.

In the Technology part of our book, the different web meeting systems and their features have already been discussed. We would like to draw your attention to the fact that in most virtual meetings, only 10-20% of the possibilities of the system are being used – chiefly because users are not aware of what the system can actually do.

CHECKLIST SPATIAL DIMENSION:

- ☑ Prepare a whiteboard for visualization
- ☑ Set up polls
- ☑ Set up break out rooms
- ☑ Have participant's list available for direct address

PRACTICAL FACILITATION TIPS:

So here are some pointers of important features:

- **Whiteboards** are used in a similar way as flip charts and online 'pin boards' and enable a different quality of interaction.
- **Using polls** speeds up decision-making processes, and/or can also be used to get a quick sounding-out of ideas and reactions from the team on a particular topic.
- **Breakout rooms** give participants the possibility to discuss questions and topics in small groups separately from the whole group and therefore enable more in-depth discussions.

CHAPTER 4 VIRTUAL MEETING FACILITATION

Sometimes a very simple activity can pay off a lot. If I have the impression that participants are getting distracted, I try to do what in a shared physical space would be called **'walking through the room'** – in virtual space, this means directly approaching each participant by name and asking for his/her opinion on the topic in question.

SOCIAL DIMENSION
GOAL:
Combining the content-related goal with the social process, taking group dynamics into account and taking advantage of team collaboration.

In order to create a team atmosphere, and also to keep people focused, it is very important to make sure you encourage interaction by planning different interventions such as icebreakers, one-to-one interaction, sharing of something personal, etc. The goal is to create an atmosphere where people are eager to share and at the same time make people feel closer to each other.

CHECKLIST SOCIAL DIMENSION:
- ☑ Choose a group structure
- ☑ Define the group composition
- ☑ Actively plan virtual subgroups
- ☑ Use pictures
- ☑ Reduce social pressure by using anonymity features

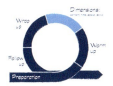

PRACTICAL FACILITATION TIPS:

- **Creating a feeling of closeness by using pictures:** Invite participants to share their picture and show what they/you look like. This helps to create trust and gives a face to a voice.

- **Reduce social pressure that limits participation:**
Use features for voting, brainstorming and reaching consensus that enable participants to be anonymous. To take some examples, polls enable a quick and anonymous feedback regarding the opinions of the group. The chat function, enabling participants to send questions privately to the facilitator only, gives team members the possibility to ask "silly" questions without feeling embarrassed or constrained in front of the whole group.

- **Actively planning virtual subgroups:** Structure the agenda, so that people can work in sub teams. Having discussions in virtual subgroups needs a bit more coordination and preparation than in a face to face meeting where you might just say: "The three of you and the three of you, please discuss this and that". Nevertheless, planning small group discussions is easily manageable. Some virtual meeting systems already offer the option of break out groups where people can have parallel working sessions and after having completed their task can join the plenary again to present their results.
If the software in use does not provide this, the facilitator could schedule parallel meeting sessions where the groups can dial in to a meeting together just for the time of the group work and then 'join back' into the main meeting room space once their shorter meeting is closed. Whatever choices are possible for you, it is advisable to change the group formats and composition during the course of longer meetings or workshops. The change in the composition of the group sometimes automatically helps create more attention to the content.

- **Choosing the right group structure:** Is it important that everyone should hear everything that is said? Or is it rather more important that everyone has sufficient time to discuss and structure their thoughts in a more intimate setting with others, and come back with a condensed, aligned and clear picture on the situation? Do participants first need to make up their mind alone, or with a partner? Depending on the answer to these questions, you would pick a different social format and group structure. The social format in terms of group size can vary from individual work, discussion in pairs, triads, small groups – or in the whole group with all meeting participants at once.

CHAPTER 4 VIRTUAL MEETING FACILITATION

GROUP STRUCTURES IN PRACTICE:

 Individual work

Pairs

Triads

 Small groups of 4 to 7

Bigger groups of 8 to 18

- **Defining the group composition:**
  After choosing the right group structure, another question is who should discuss which topics and with whom? Supposing that meeting participants share different views and opinions on a certain topic, it might be advisable to think of the composition of the discussion groups. Sometimes it is better to have people of the same opinion in the same group, which helps them to strengthen their standpoint. In other situations it might be important to soften 'hardened' positions or escalate certain issues.

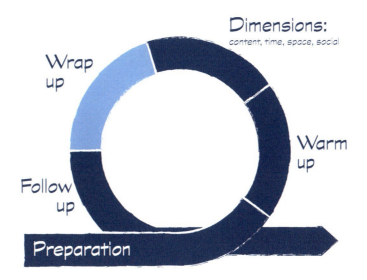

WRAP UP

Supposing that your meeting has been effective and the last agenda point has been dealt with just on time. The facilitator is just about to thank everyone for attending the meeting and wants to point out some last things. While doing so, he realises that everyone has already left the meeting and he is there alone in virtual space. This actually happens quite often – at least from what we have experienced! In order to avoid that unpleasant experience, it makes sense to actively plan the end of a meeting and save some time for a proper wrap up, with everyone saying goodbye before they disappear.

GOAL:

Joint action orientation on decisions made and tasks assigned.
Communicating one voice: Joint definition of what and when decisions or actions will be communicated to people affected by decisions.

CHAPTER 4 VIRTUAL MEETING FACILITATION

CHECKLIST WRAP UP

- ☑ Wrap up content and commitment: summary, to-do list, commitments, follow-up dates?
- ☑ The next meeting: goals, topics, facilitation?
- ☑ Communication: main messages, mail, press release, video message?
- ☑ Feedback /learning points/professional and personal development of team members, overall development of the whole team?

PRACTICAL FACILITATION TIPS:

There are different parts of wrap ups:

- **Wrap up content and commitment:** This includes a summary of the meeting results including decisions and to-dos and a joint commitment by the meeting participants. The big advantage of virtual meetings is that the results can easily be documented visually and visibly – in front of all participants - and are therefore transparent for all. Together with the to do list, the follow up dates should also be defined at this stage.

- **Follow-Up Dates:** Definition of goals, topics and "the special points" for the next meeting. If the moderation or facilitation role is rotated, the moderator for the next meeting is assigned.

- **Communication:** Definition of the 'content message' that needs to be communicated. This could be as varied as the joint definition of main messages for personal communication, a jointly drafted mail, a press release, or a video message.

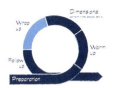

- **Feedback/Learning/Professional Development:** This includes personal feedback or a joint reflection of the meeting quality or the overall development of the team.
Typical questions we often use in the end of a web meeting are communicated through a poll feature, and would include:
"How satisfied am I with the result of this meeting (1-5)?
How satisfied am I with the quality of discussion in the meeting (1-5)?
How satisfied am I with our development as a team (1-5)?"
And then, of course, some discussion and analysis of the poll results.

- **'Emotional' closing:** Next to the content-related actions it might be a good intervention to also think of an emotional close to the meeting. In other words, one that reflects people's feelings and state of mind, especially if the meeting explored conflicts or emotional topics. If one of the goals of the meetings is to establish a good working atmosphere between the meeting participants or to build a team, it is advisable to also include personal, relationship-building activities both in the warm up and wrap up of a meeting. The more participants share, the more they learn about each other and the more trust can be established. And, as we have suggested throughout this book, if trust is there then better team performance usually follows.

EXAMPLES OF WRAP UP ACTIVITIES:

POLL:

Polls as wrap up activities can be used very quickly for getting a 'temperature check' of people's needs and reactions, and only require two minutes at the end of the meeting. They can also be followed by a discussion about the results and possible next steps in consequence of those results, which would require an additional 5-10 minutes of the meeting.

Some examples for poll questions are:

- How satisfied am I with the result of this meeting?
- How clear are the next steps and action points to me?

CHAPTER 4 VIRTUAL MEETING FACILITATION

USING VOICE:

Finish the same way as you started, by having everyone make a statement. This can be very quick or more in depth, depending on your available time and the question/s you ask. Some examples of a 'vocal' wrap up activity include asking everyone, in turn:

- Give one word as your résumé of this meeting?
- One word expressing with which thought/feeling/emotion you are leaving this meeting right now?
- One closing sentence from everyone?
- Have all your expectations been fulfilled?
- What are you (most) looking forward to in the implementation of today's decisions….?
- What is your major take-away from this meeting?
- What was especially great about this meeting/today's topics/today's results?
- What will you communicate to your team members about this meeting?

CHAT BOX:

The meeting is already five minutes over time, and you know that people need to leave and won't have time for a long wrap up activity. So just ask them quickly to post their summary comment, possibly in response to a question like one of those shown above, in the chat box before they leave. This gives you a quick sounding of the mood of the group and provides some possible structure and an orientation for the next meeting.

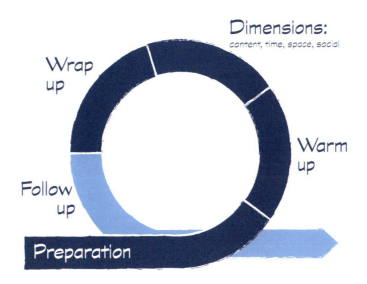

FOLLOW UP

A meeting can be efficient and fun but it will be without impact if there is no implementation of the measures and action points that have been agreed following it. There are a range of virtual collaboration platforms and systems in place to help you track the agreed tasks, and many organisations have their own individual SharePoint system for that.

GOAL:

Consistent implementation and transparency on the progress

CHAPTER 4 VIRTUAL MEETING FACILITATION

CHECKLIST FOLLOW UP

- ☑ Minutes
- ☑ Implementation teams
- ☑ Implementation tracking

PRACTICAL FACILITATION TIPS:

For the role of the meeting owner or facilitator, here are the aspects of the follow up that are important to consider:

- **Minutes:** One part of the follow up process is producing the meeting minutes, including the main decisions and action points. These can be distributed right after the meeting.

- **Implementation teams:** Often implementation teams continue working on specific tasks in smaller working groups and sometimes need coordination and project management support.

- **Tracking:** If tasks have been agreed in a meeting and are never followed up, this might either mean that they were not really important or that there is something going wrong in the project management. This could at least be addressed in the beginning of a follow up meeting, and considered when new action points are assigned, since this might lead to a reprioritisation of tasks and deadlines.

Virtual meetings are one of the most convenient and effective ways for human beings to collaborate in a digitalised, globalised economic culture, and as such, they still have a lot of under-used potential.

Even as we write, the world moves on, and we feel sure that in just a few years' time the systems available to run virtual meetings will have many additional features which bring virtual collaboration to an even higher level of quality in communication, convenience and effectiveness. Until that happens, we invite you to think of how to use your meetings in the most valuable way, clarifying and supporting the specific goals you want to achieve in each meeting, and including ways of involving everyone in the most appropriate ways.

CONCLUSION

LOOKING BACK

to the time when we started writing the book and getting involved in the topic of virtual leadership and virtual teams, we can see how things have developed at high speed and how "virtual reality" is becoming more and more part of our daily lives.

We remember organising our first webinars back in 2009, where people would join just to test out the (back then) new technology. And now we have clients sending out virtual meeting invitations around the clock, and it has become "normal" to do certain kind of work virtually. All of this is very exciting to notice - how the virtual world is becoming part of businesses (and private lives) globally, and how increasingly sophisticated technology and a developing 'mind-set' regarding virtual work is making it more and more accessible, whether you are an independent consultant or trainer working alone, or a team leader at any level in a multi-national corporation.

It could be that you, our reader, have been leading a virtual team for some years already without thinking too much about the consequences of "virtual" in your leadership style and skills, but knowing that some practical tips that can be easily implemented within your team will be very useful to you. Or perhaps, in contrast, you are not yet really needing to work virtually, or to facilitate a virtual meeting, but you see the necessity to learn more about it - because eventually you know you will have to deal with this topic.

Whichever kind of reader you are, our goal in writing this book has been to make the "virtual world" real and accessible for everybody – from the dynamic virtual expert who searches for new inspiration, to the less virtually experienced reader who may be feeling a bit lost in the complex world of communication and leadership in cyber space.

LOOKING AHEAD

Writing about trends on such a fast-moving topic as the new way of working that virtual collaboration offers us is quite a challenging task. In the time that will elapse between writing these lines and you reading them, all kinds of new on-line collaboration tools are likely to have been launched, perhaps bringing a dazzling variety of new features to try out, and sparking new insights and awareness on virtual work in general out there in the business world.

It is evident that virtual collaboration is already "business as usual" for many people and will become even more important in the future. It is no longer a topic that is seen as relevant only for modern, forward-looking companies and the so called "millennial" businesses, it is rapidly becoming a core topic of interest for anyone working across distance, either nationally or internationally.

Our company's annual global survey, conducted with more than 400 managers of leading international companies, has shown that digital transformation is perceived as one of the top 5 challenges in 2016 and now therefore plays an important role on the leadership agenda.[34]

In addition, Forbes[35] cites studies from Gartner and Forrester stating that "Digital transformation will become the key strategic thrust for most CEOs. In 2016, CEOs will make a concerted effort to integrate the various digital initiatives across the business and create a clear digital vision that shows how the business will deliver revenue-generating digital experiences".

Looking at these comments it comes obvious that digital working – efficient and effective virtual collaboration – is already something rather more significant than an aspect of business which offers competitive advantage and a low-cost, modern way of working to team leaders right up to CEO level. Rather, it is well on its way to becoming a recognised, core element of business success the world over.

We hope that you enjoyed reading our compilation of different perspectives on the topic of virtual collaboration and gained some inspiration for your own work as a leader, team member, consultant or trainer. "Keep developing" is one of the main drivers of our work, so we aim to also keep researching and working on this fascinating, emerging topic of virtual leadership. Please look out for regular updates and insights of our discoveries, and how to apply them, on our website www.makingvirtualreal.com. We would be delighted to receive your feedback, comments and discoveries in turn.

We wish you, our reader, the greatest success in "making virtual real"!

Keep developing.

---

34 Doujak Global Survey 2016: http://www.doujak.eu/insights-publications/the-doujak-global-survey-2016/ (seen January 2016)
35 http://www.forbes.com/sites/gilpress/2015/12/06/6-predictions-about-the-future-of-digital-transformation/ (seen January 2016)

REFERENCES

1 Doujak Global Survey 2016: http://www.doujak.eu/insights-publications/the-doujak-global-survey-2016/(seen January 2016)

2 G. Caulat, "Virtual Leadership", The Ashridge Journal, Autumn 2006.

3 Christopher Mabey and Sally Caird 1999 Building Team Effectiveness Open University, Milton Keynes,

ISBN 0-7492-9553-8, Page 7 ff.

4 https://en.wikipedia.org/wiki/Virtual_team (14.7.2015)

5 Caulat G., (2010) Virtual Leadership: Rethinking Virtual Teams.

6 Neeley T., "Getting Cross-Cultural Teamwork Right, Harvard Business Review, 2015

7 Google search "What is Culture?": 1,450,000,000 search results on 12.10.2015

8 Image Iceberg Model: http://www.differencedifferently.edu.au/defining_identities/part_1a.php 4

9 Hammerich K., Lewis R., "Fish Can't See Water: How National Cultures Can Make or Break Your Corporate Strategy", Wiley, 2013

10 Meyer E., "One Reason Cross-Cultural Small Talk Is So Tricky", Harvard Business Review, 2014, p 23

11 Report "Leading International Virtual Teams: Challenges and best practices of virtual teams", Viviana Rojas de Amon, 2012

12 Molinsky A., "The Big Challenge of American Small Talk", Harvard Business Review, 2013

13 E. Meyer, "One Reason Cross-Cultural Small Talk Is So Tricky", Harvard Business Review, 2014

14 Hall E. T:, "Beyond Culture", 1976

15 Meyer E., "How To Say 'This Is Crap' In Different Cultures", Harvard Business Review, 2014

16 Lewis R., How Different Cultures Understand Time", Business Insider, 2014

17 Fogelberg F., Tavanyar J., et al "Live connections: Virtual Facilitation for High Engagement and Powerful Learning", Nomadic, 2015, p. 166

18 Crandell C., "What Does Trust Have To Do With Anything?", Forbes, 2012

19 Greenberg P.S., H. Greenberg R., Lederer Antonucci Y., "Creating and Sustaining Trust in Virtual Teams", Business Horizons (2007) 50, 325–333

20 Brake T., "Where in the World is my Team?", Jossey-Bass, 2008

21 Meyer E., "The Culture Map: Breaking Through the Invisible Boundaries of Global Business", Public Affairs, 2014, p. 189

22 Hofstede G., Hofstede G.H., Minkov M., "Cultures and Organisations: Software of the Mind", 3rd Edition, McGraw-Hill USA, 2010

23 Duarte D. L., Tennant Snyder N., "Mastering Virtual Teams: Strategies Tools and Techniques that Succeed, Jossey-Bass, 2006 p 149-153

24 Hofstede G., Hofstede G.H., Minkov M., "Cultures and Organisations: Software of the Mind", 3rd Edition, McGraw-Hill USA, 2010

25 Lencioni P. M., "The Five Dysfunctions of a Team: A Leadership Fable" 2002

26 Duarte D. L., Tennant Snyder N., "Mastering Virtual Teams: Strategies Tools and Techniques that Succeed", Jossey-Bass, 3rd edition 2006, p. 139-143

27 G. Caulat, "Virtual Leadership", The Ashridge Journal, Autumn 2006.

28 A. Doujak, B. Heitger, Harte Schnitte Neues Wachstum: Wandel in Volatilen Zeiten. Die Macht der Zahlen und die Logik der Gefühle im Change Management, 2. Edition, 2014, p. 205-206

29 F. Fogelberg, J. Tavanyar, et al "Live Connections: Virtual Facilitation for High Engagement and Powerful Learning", Nomadic, 2015

30 Harvard Business Review, Gretchen Gavett, What People are Really Doing When They're on a Conference Call, August 2014.

31 Harvard Business Review, Elizabeth Grace Saunders, Do You Really Need to Hold That Meeting? March 2015.

32 https://en.wikipedia.org/wiki/Picture_superiority_effect

33 http://www.online-stopwatch.com/full-screen-online-countdown

34 Doujak Global Survey 2016: http://www.doujak.eu/insights-publications/the-doujak-global-survey-2016/(seen January 2016)

35 http://www.forbes.com/sites/gilpress/2015/12/06/6-predictions-about-the-future-of-digital-transformation/(seen January 2016)

FIGURES

Fig. 1: Advantages of Virtual Teams. © Doujak Corporate Development

Fig. 2: Traditional Teams vs. Virtual Teams Challenges.© Doujak Corporate Development

Fig. 3: Four Types of Distance Affecting Virtual Teams © Doujak Corporate Development

Fig. 4: Aspects of Remote Leadership Virtual Team Leaders Should Consider When Managing Task and Relationship-Related Challenges. © Doujak Corporate Development

Fig. 5: Individual Culture Model. © Elisa Alberto

Fig. 6: "Passport" visualization of the culture model

Fig. 7: Meyer E., "The Culture Map: Breaking Through The Invisible Boundaries of Global

REFERENCES

Business", Public Affairs, 2014 P. 72

Fig. 8: Scale Exercise "Preferences on Giving and Receiving Negative Feedback", © Doujak Corporate Development.

Fig. 9: Source: www.ecute.eu/theory/synthetic-cultures/

FIg.: 10: Competences and Skills for Successful Virtual Leaders. © Doujak Corporate Development

Fig. 11: Dynamics in Leadership Facilitation. © Doujak Corporate Development.

Fig. 12: Dynamics in Leadership Facilitation. © Doujak Corporate Development.

Fig. 13 Doujak Virtual Team Performance Model © Doujak Corporate Development.

Fig. 14: Source: Nomadic training "Virtual Facilitation Skills"

Fig. 15: Meeting facilitation loop © Dooujak Corporate Development

ILLUSTRATIONS AND PHOTOGRAPHIES

p. 24 Different types of distance © Susanne Hun

p. 32 Individual, team, organisation icons © Susanne Hun

p. 36 Iceberg infographic © blauananas – modified by Susanne Hun

p. 39 Iceberg infographic © blauananas – modified by Susanne Hun

p. 41 Illustration of Individual Culture Model by Elisa Alberto © Susanne Hun

p. 43 Passport" visualization of the culture model © Elisa Alberto

p. 44 Culture Model Glasses © Susanne Hun

p. 45 Group Of Business © rawpixel.com – modified by Susanne Hun

p. 51 Overlapping conversations © Susanne Hun

p. 101 Draw the World ©

p. 115 Doujak Virtual Team Performance Model illustrated by Susanne Hun

p. 144/145 Sketch Management Concept © macrovector – modified by Susanne Hun

p. 149 Information Graphic Illustration by Susanne Hun

p. 165/166 Smiley faces icons set. Vector illustration © pakkad; Weather icons set. Vector illustration © pakkad; Battery icons © Susanne Hun

p. 172 Road and mist, Lofoten islands, Norway © Iakov Kalinin; Dangerous blurry driving car in the rainy weather © robsonphoto – modified by Susanne Hun; Winter © trendobjects; Very bumpy road in hot summer © THPStock; Broken Road © ollirg; Traffic jam © bibi

Made in the USA
Charleston, SC
01 June 2016